Constructing an Online

PROFESSIONAL
LEARNING
NETWORK

for **SCHOOL UNITY** and
STUDENT ACHIEVEMENT

We dedicate this book to our families, who have offered never-ending support and encouragement to us.

Constructing an Online

PROFESSIONAL LEARNING NETWORK

for SCHOOL UNITY and STUDENT ACHIEVEMENT

ROBIN THOMPSON   LAURIE KITCHIE   ROBERT GAGNON

A Joint Publication

CORWIN
A SAGE Company

FOR INFORMATION:

Corwin

A SAGE Company

2455 Teller Road

Thousand Oaks, California 91320

(800) 233-9936

Fax: (800) 417-2466

www.corwin.com

SAGE Ltd.

1 Oliver's Yard

55 City Road

London EC1Y 1SP

United Kingdom

SAGE India Pvt. Ltd.

B 1/I 1 Mohan Cooperative Industrial Area

Mathura Road, New Delhi 110 044

India

SAGE Asia-Pacific Pte. Ltd.

33 Pekin Street #02-01

Far East Square

Singapore 048763

Acquisitions Editor: Arnis Burvikovs

Associate Editor: Desirée A. Bartlett

Editorial Assistant: Kim Greenberg

Project Editor: Veronica Stapleton

Copy Editor: Alan Cook

Typesetter: C&M Digitals (P) Ltd.

Proofreader: Dennis W. Webb

Indexer: Gloria Tierney

Cover Designer: Michael Dubowe

Permissions Editor: Karen Ehrmann

Printed in the United States of America

Library of Congress Cataloging-in-Publication Data

Thompson, Robin, 1960-

Constructing an online professional learning network for school unity and student achievement/Robin Thompson, Laurie Kitchie, Robert Gagnon.

A Joint Publication with Learning Forward

p. cm.
Includes bibliographical references and index.

ISBN 978-1-4129-9492-7 (pbk.)

1. Professional learning communities. 2. Teachers—In-service training. 3. Educational technology. I. Kitchie, Laurie. II. Gagnon, Robert, 1967- III. Title.

LB1731.T48 2011
371.33—dc23   2011025067

This book is printed on acid-free paper.

11 12 13 14 15 10 9 8 7 6 5 4 3 2 1

Contents

All of the resources described and presented in this book are also available at www.your professionallearningnetwork.com.

List of Figures

Preface

Getting the Big Picture

The goal of this book is to define a professional learning network (PLN), detail each of its components, and demonstrate how your school can increase its focus on technology, communication, achievement, and professional development with the successful design and implementation of its own PLN. Our conception of a PLN expands the current notion of a professional learning *community* while simultaneously addressing and providing solutions to some of the oft-stated weaknesses of professional learning communities, including lack of time, resources, and space.

How the Concept of a PLN Came Into Focus

The impetus for our school's establishment of a PLN came from a district curricular mandate. Our county had recently adopted a core curriculum in which content teachers were required to teach the same content at the same pace while administering the same assessments. We knew that implementation of this new core curriculum was going to be a challenge for most and a paradigm shift for some, so we began to look for a platform that would ensure teacher success, offer a space for collaboration, supply necessary resources while differentiating diverse levels of need, and provide a nonthreatening environment in which teachers could learn at their own pace.

Regardless of whether you agree or disagree with the implementation of specific directives and mandates, a PLN can be useful in addressing the complexities that coincide with a new initiative and scaffold both teachers and students toward success by providing ample opportunities to access and share resources, acquire expertise, and engage in professional conversations. The sustainability of a PLN appealed to us because, as all educators have experienced, there are frequent mandates, initiatives, and changes in education. A PLN is able to communicate these changes, incorporate them into its existing structure, and provide additional resources and information about them. A PLN can grow with its members and accommodate needs in school communities with a few simple clicks.

WHAT TO EXPECT IN THIS BOOK

We have designed our chapters to address each of the elements that contribute to *our* PLN and to provide explicit details and sequential steps in order for *your* school community to successfully design a PLN that addresses your specific needs, ultimately leading to increased student achievement.

At the beginning of each chapter, we explain the *why* behind our reasons for choosing to include that particular component on ManateeLearn, the designated website for our PLN. We then provide a "snapshot" of the process we used in designing how that component would look in our PLN. Next, a "bird's-eye view" is given in the form of a list of factors for you to consider as you begin planning the blueprints for your own PLN. Each chapter ends with a quick review and all of the resources, graphic organizers, and planning guides mentioned in the chapter.

Chapter 1, "Focus on a Professional Learning Network," defines a PLN. It explains why a PLN is a wise choice for a school community. The chapter also provides some straightforward recommendations that a school at any level (elementary, middle, or high school) can put into place to begin the process of designing its own PLN to meet the needs of its school community.

Chapter 2, "Zooming in on Leadership," introduces a tiered leadership structure that enabled our school administration to share the roles and responsibilities in designing, building, and implementing our PLN. Empowering additional leaders in our school community gave people a voice in the planning stages and produced more ownership in a variety of aspects of our PLN.

Chapter 3, "Going Digital: Infusing Technology Into a PLN," provides a review of how we built our PLN and lists steps to guide you through the process of building your own PLN.

Chapter 4, "Landscape for Communication of Information," gives a broad overview of how we've used our PLN as a platform for increased communication among members of our school community. We detail how we set up our PLN to communicate to all faculty members simultaneously regarding curricular mandates, school initiatives, and professional development opportunities. We are able to convey information, provide feedback, post data and plans, and offer resources on a platform that all members of our school community can access.

Chapter 5, "Framing Curriculum and Instruction," provides explanations for the curricular pieces found in our PLN, including each of the facets of our common instructional framework that supports curriculum standards across all contents. As a result of our common instructional model, we have a schoolwide focus on best practices in our instructional strategies, daily targeted instruction aimed at areas of weakness, and daily informal assessments to monitor progress and achievement of students.

Chapter 6, "Exposures to Learning," discusses with specificity the learning processes and opportunities made possible by our PLN, focusing on both the face-to-face and the online components of the professional development offered. Our PLN addresses diverse levels of need by providing online differentiated professional development resources that can be used at any time and according to need while still enabling us to address the teachers face to face for explicit instruction in the uses of the online components and for deep discussions of student and teacher growth and needs.

Chapter 7, "Begin Your Focus with Eight Steps," includes a review of all the steps necessary to build your own PLN. There is a short description of each of the eight steps along with a detailed worksheet to help you get started.

Chapter 8, "Adding Perspective: Viewing a PLN with a New Lens," discusses various achievements we accomplished during the first year of implementation of our PLN and considers next steps.

WHY WE WROTE THIS BOOK

Our network provides a space for our schoolwide goals to be shared, discussed, supported, and amended. As a result of a needs assessment, current data, and curriculum mandates, our school community chose to focus on some specific goals in the belief that doing so would increase student achievement. At the conclusion of this book, it will be evident that our network frames and supports our school community while providing a space for collegiality and communication among and within our departments; thus serving to unify our school community with common goals, learning, and a network designed around the needs of its members.

Our goal in writing this book is to provide school communities with a general framework from which they can design a PLN that will meet their particular needs, along with some practical steps to take in order to ensure the success of their PLN. Our own school community's establishment and use of a PLN will serve as the model from which we will share experiences, show examples, and give advice.

Our PLN can be found at www.ManateeLearn.com, but because it is a secure site you will not be able to access much of what we discuss in this book. In order for you to be able to access the information and documents found in this book and to see examples of how we have arranged our PLN, we have set up a sample PLN at www.yourprofessionallearning network.com. You will find all the resources plus sample pages at this site.

Our hope is that each PLN resulting from this book becomes a viable and practical tool with which to meet the specific and diverse needs of your school community.

Acknowledgments

We are fortunate to work with a fabulous group of professionals at Manatee High School. They were willing, flexible, and innovative throughout the process of building, implementing, and revising our PLN. Without their contributions, our PLN might still be an unrealized dream. Thank you to each teacher and administrator who has logged on, uploaded plans, participated in forums, found resources, gone through a module, used student data, projected student exemplars, and everything else. Thank you.

PUBLISHER'S ACKNOWLEDGMENTS

Corwin would like to thank the following individuals for their editorial insight and guidance:

Barbara Cavanah, Coordinator/Supervisor
Instructional Technology
Monroe County School District
Key West, Florida

Tania Dymkowski, Instructional Strategist
Science Hall Elementary School
Hayes Consolidated Independent School District
Kyle, Texas

Cheryl Steele Oakes, Teacher
Wells High School
Wells, Maine

Lyndon Oswald, Principal
Sandcreek Middle School
Ammon, Idaho

Renee Peoples, Teacher
West Elementary School
Bryson City, North Carolina

Linda Sarver, Teacher (retired)
Westview Elementary School
Excelsior Springs School District
Excelsior Springs, Missouri

About the Authors

Photo by Kris Gause

Robin Thompson With a degree in curriculum and instruction that includes an emphasis in literacy, Robin is especially interested in struggling adolescent readers. Although she started her work in elementary education, she has subsequently taught at many levels (middle school, high school, and college) and is currently the curriculum coordinator at Manatee High School. Prior to this position, she was the reading coach and an intensive reading teacher at the high school. Her research interests include struggling adolescent readers' increased achievement in fluency, vocabulary, and comprehension, so the process of designing, building, and launching a PLN focused on increased student achievement was an exciting opportunity for her.

Robert Gagnon Currently the principal of Manatee High School in Bradenton, Florida, Bob and his team have had the honor of bringing a D-rated high school on the Florida Department of Education school rating scale to an A rating. He has worked diligently to demonstrate leadership and believes firmly that through teacher empowerment and the modeling of effective guidance any school climate can be transformed and improved. He and his team have truly accomplished a monumental task; they will continue to build on this achievement and make revisions to meet the needs of both teachers and students at Manatee High School.

Laurie Kitchie A graduate of the University of Florida in educational technology, Laurie embraces the concept of connectivism when it comes to educating adolescent and adult learners alike. In today's digital environment, it is more important than ever to explore the biology of the human mind as well as the tools that exist outside the human mind that aid in learning. Laurie has experience teaching both English and reading in Grades 6 through 12. At the present time she is an assistant principal at Manatee High School in Bradenton, Florida. Her work developing a PLN for the school has provided an exciting and rare experience of taking an idea and bringing it to fruition. The team has synthesized various levels of expertise to develop a PLN that has already exceeded their initial expectations and that can continue to grow with the rapidly transforming learning environment.

Photo by Kris Gause

CHAPTER 1

Focusing on a Professional Learning Network

ManateeLearn has been an effective resource for my professional development. As a result of the site, I have been able to have access to resources that are beneficial to my instructional planning as well as collaborate and network with other faculty members from various content areas. The 24-hour access to the site accommodates my planning time and is accessible to me on weekends and nights. I have benefited from the instructional resources that are available and am confident that if I have a question that I am pondering, I can be certain that I can find resolution and support from ManateeLearn.

—Kellie Viera, reading teacher, mentor

WHAT IS A PROFESSIONAL LEARNING NETWORK?

A professional learning network (PLN) is a platform (either online, face-to-face, or blended) from which professionals (in our case, educators) learn to become more effective practitioners by collaborating and studying with colleagues and other experts, focusing on student data, learning styles, and achievement, while self-reflecting and revising instructional practices and pedagogical stances in order to better meet students' needs. A secondary goal and natural outgrowth of successful PLNs is the unification of stakeholders in a school community that results from increased collegiality, open communication, and common goals. Finally, inherent in the setup of a PLN, space is provided to address the complexities that coincide with any new district, state, or national initiative or directive and to scaffold both teachers and students toward success by providing ample opportunities to post new information, access and share resources, acquire expertise, and engage in professional conversations.

WHY A PLN FOCUS?

Professional learning communities (PLCs) are designed to promote similar goals and values, and to foster collaboration by having participants work together using inquiry and applied practice. A PLN broadens this by embracing the goals of a PLC and infusing overarching themes that benefit the entire school environment. In a sense, a PLN is a planned development of a PLC, much like a planned neighborhood development. Each group has its own individual goals that feed into the larger and often more complicated goals of the PLN. By using a planned network approach, even the most diverse groups can achieve success in bringing their individual ideas to embrace the goals of the entire school.

Our PLN expands the current notion of a professional learning community, in that it

- Provides a platform from which to articulate and communicate the school's mission, vision, and goals to all community members (administrators, teachers, and staff)
- Creates opportunities for shared leadership by serving as a schoolwide depository to which all stakeholders may contribute and from which they may benefit

- Delivers differentiated professional development for collective and individual learning and instruction
- Ensures opportunities for all voices to be heard by building participatory forums
- Provides space for posting student data, publishing the resulting school initiatives, and collaborating with colleagues to determine best teaching practices with regard to common curriculum expectations
- Celebrates shared practices by housing and making available model lessons, presentations, and student products to all teachers

Our PLN simultaneously addresses and provides solutions to some of the frequently stated weaknesses of PLCs: insufficient time, resources, and space. It resolves these issues by communicating information, posting data, and providing professional development asynchronously, thus enabling the stakeholders to access it at their convenience, revisit it upon need, choose topics of interest, all while requiring no additional physical space or cost for resources.

A PLN also resembles a compilation of *personal* learning networks, if one thinks of the school community as the individual, linking PLCs, providing the latest feeds on political decisions that affect school communities, and posting common objectives. PLNs, or personal learning networks or environments, operate like a second brain in the sense that they allow an individual to synthesize information from a variety of sources in order to stay informed about the large amount of information that is available daily over the web. A person can run a calendar, track specific blogs and wiki pages, stay up-to-date with national and global information, and communicate socially through e-mail, forums, and instant messaging, all on one site that he or she has tailored to meet specific goals and objectives. By using a personal learning network or environment, less time is spent searching for information that aligns with set goals and objectives. In addition, the quality of information used to make decisions is heightened because unrelated sources are filtered appropriately.

We have incorporated all of the advantages of a personal learning network into our PLN in order to streamline, organize, and prioritize the onslaught of information available each day in the field of education. We have an interactive calendar, links to our databases and online grade book, resources for professional development that focus on research-based best practices, folders that are populated with lessons and student samples, and forums to communicate with other members of our school community. It's as if our school has a *personal* learning network that only hosts our professional interests; hence, our *professional* learning network.

Finally, the term *networked learning communities*, coined by Stoll and Louis, could also be associated with our PLN, because schools were united online as they developed community. We take this networking a step further, in that networking takes place in both face-to-face encounters and online. We especially want to emphasize the importance of the networking that occurs face-to-face. This is the time during which rapport is built, relationships are established, and we become a community of learners.

SNAPSHOT OF *OUR* PLN

Our PLN is comprised of five main elements, each serving a specific purpose in contributing toward our school community's goal of increasing student achievement. The entire network is adaptable, in that the components each offer diverse options, in any given order, for a variety of levels of stakeholders, thus meeting the needs of many individuals with a multitude of methods, time frames, learning styles, and goals. The main parts are

Technology. We chose a blended platform, as we have a large and diverse faculty with varying levels of knowledge about technology and its applications. This decision was based on the results of our needs assessment and technology survey, the technology resources available at our school, and the recommendation of our technology committee. Technology

Figure 1.1   Professional Learning Network

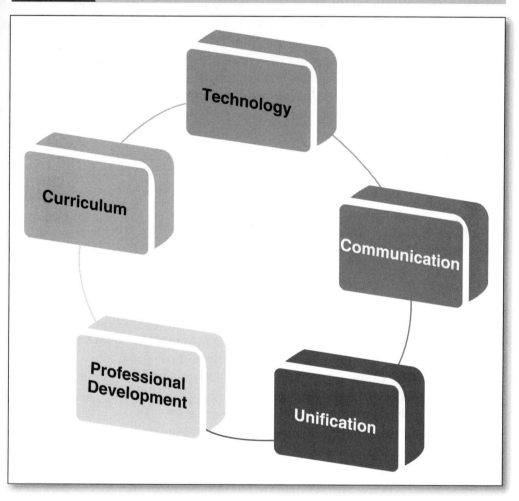

has two roles: it is a tool used to provide networked learning, and it provides teachers with scaffolding and experience in using higher level technology than that to which they are accustomed, which should lead to increased use of technology within the classroom.

Communication. Our PLN is used as a hub of communication for our school. We are able to communicate school goals and initiatives, provide resources, offer student samples and teachers' presentations, and post data. Our site has become a source of information regarding our school community. In addition, we linked the already existing PLCs at our school with our small learning communities and academies, thus using our PLN to serve as a unifying agent within and across our school community.

Curriculum. Since increased student achievement was our overarching goal, we developed a daily instructional framework based on best practices and current research findings that would incorporate the requirements of our newly adopted core curriculum, while still serving our stakeholders' needs. We then introduced this framework to the school community, both online and face-to-face. We created folders to support our daily framework that could house teachers' lessons, samples of students' work, and assessments used.

Professional Development. As many of the technology and curriculum pieces were new, complex, and multifaceted, we anticipated a need for differentiated professional development around a variety of topics, from which teachers could choose to glean an overview or to delve deeply and access additional resources, all while participating in professional conversations and reflecting on instructional practices. The professional development features are made up of a broad range of topics, are offered asynchronously, and occur both online and face-to-face.

Unification (bringing it all together). Each element in our PLN addresses specific needs of our school community. Each is linked to data. Each is aligned with the national, state, and district mandates to which we are required to adhere. Our school's focus and goals are reflected in every aspect. Unification focuses on tying together all the individual pieces in order to create an inclusive community.

Initial Steps in the Design of Our PLN

Some initial data gathering was necessary to inform our leadership teams of current perceptions and status of our school community. In order to construct a sustainable PLN, accuracy in our data collection and analysis was important. Furthermore, our long- and short-term goals were determined by our data, so valid data from several sources were used to test and confirm hypotheses about current school needs. Following are some of the data we used to begin the discussions of what our PLN would look like. Although this is just a part of the data we used, it served us well in the beginning stages.

Technology Survey

We have a diverse faculty with regard to use and knowledge of technology. The goals of the technology survey we created were twofold. We wanted to find out the stakeholders' (administrators, teachers, and staff) perceptions of our schoolwide technology needs, based on what they visualized as an ideal technology environment; but we also hoped to find out each stakeholder's level of knowledge and what scaffolds would best lead toward increased technology knowledge, use, and comfort.

We analyzed the data from the survey and created two lists of priorities: first, a list that outlined and specified technology resources that we hoped to acquire over time; and second, a list that set out a series of levels of knowledge and detailed what each level included, with a corresponding number that indicated the number of stakeholders who requested more knowledge about specific programs, classroom uses, and hardware. This list enabled us to begin to plan for the technology component of our professional development program and to address some of the stakeholders' needs immediately. We have included the technology survey (Resource A) that we used, in order to provide a guideline as you enter into the process of identifying your technology goals.

Needs Assessment

Because we are a large public high school with approximately 2,175 students and over 100 teachers, it is nearly impossible to achieve consensus on every issue that requires attention during the school year. Administering a needs assessment gives each person a voice while also providing an adequate amount of data that can be analyzed, prioritized, and organized so that it can be presented back to the faculty as a framework from which an action plan can be more readily designed and implemented. The needs assessment that we designed for our uses is included (Resource B). We have also included a worksheet that we developed to help us analyze and prioritize the results of the needs assessment (Resource C).

In order for the performance of administrators, teachers, and students to improve, a number of concerns need to be acknowledged and addressed prior to and during the implementation of objectives. As we started planning how to reach our first-year goals, we knew we needed to provide a multitude of supports that would be regarded as useful by the members of our school community; but until we administered and analyzed our needs assessment, we were not completely aware of our stakeholders' perceptions of our schoolwide weaknesses.

Goals and Objectives

Our initial checklist and goal-setting chart served as an outline in establishing concrete long-term goals with short-term steps. It also gave our team an opportunity to brainstorm as we completed it by filling in details that corresponded to our needs and objectives. A blank template similar to the one with which we began this process is included to be filled in with the appropriate areas of focus for your particular school community (Resource E). A copy of a portion of our completed chart is also included, in case it would be helpful for you to examine the one we used initially to track our progress and monitor our adherence to the needs of the stakeholders (Resource F).

Long-Term Goals

Because we wanted to ensure that our efforts would result in achievement of our goals, we developed a strategic calendar to clarify the steps toward success. Because change takes time, our three-year plan allowed all stakeholders ample time to embrace the new curriculum, technology, and online learning processes.

Our three-year plan became, in actuality, a three-tiered system in which the focus became more targeted each year. The goal of the first year was to address our needs at the school level, while year two shifted the focus to the classroom, and finally the third year addressed the needs at the desk level (students). Our flexible long-term goals were representative of our overarching hopes for the future of our PLN. They were as follows:

Year 1: School Level

- Design a PLN that addresses specific needs of our school community.
- Familiarize teachers and administrators with an educational management system and provide scaffolding for the technology skills needed to use our PLN successfully.
- Have each teacher use our PLN regularly for online collaboration and asynchronous learning and sharing of information.
- Populate folders so they will be useful in providing sample lessons, lesson plans, sample student work, presentations, graphic organizers, professional development resources, departmental kickoffs, and other information.
- Provide a go-to area for access to new national, state, and district mandates and access to secure student data.
- Unite PLCs within the school environment to support common schoolwide goals.

Year 2: Classroom Level

- Continue to address needs of stakeholders by continuously monitoring the use of the PLN at the school level and consistently evaluate the usefulness of its components. Make improvements based on these data.

- Strengthen teachers' instructional practices by encouraging their consistent use of all applicable populated folders' contents, including lesson plans, lessons, presentations, graphic organizers, daily assessments, etc. Continue to add to each folder to increase the resources for teachers and rigor for students.

- Rely more heavily on the site, and begin to introduce online modules for professional development.

- Gather evidence that teachers adhere to and use common instructional goals found in daily classroom instructional models and strategies, and continue to monitor impact on achievement.

- The face-to-face piece of our blended professional network funnels to the classroom level, where the teachers learn to embed the uses of the two-way platform in their instructional practices.

Year 3: Desk Level

- Continue to address needs of stakeholders by continuously monitoring the use of the PLN at both the school and classroom levels and consistently evaluating their components. Make improvements based on these data.

- Provide a student platform as a sister platform to the teacher platform. Begin to introduce the use of a blended learning environment into classrooms, so that teachers use the educational management system as their own vehicle toward improved instructional practices.

- Increase the use of the information platform and add a two-way platform where students collaborate with each other.

- The face-to-face piece of our blended professional network funnels to the desk level, where the students learn to embed the uses of the two-way platform in their collaboration and communication with peers.

Short-Term Goals

We used the framework of our long-term goals to contextualize and detail our short-term goals. Once we decided on the specific short-term steps necessary to attain the long-term objectives, we were able to develop a timeline for achievement of our goals, thus building in a progress-monitoring device in which accountability was embedded.

Our overarching goal is always to enhance student performance. Our hope with the development of our PLN was to empower both teachers and students by increasing achievement of all stakeholder groups using research-based instructional strategies. This was a far-reaching goal and could include everything from celebrating a teacher's successful electronic uploading of lesson plans to facilitating a high-level discussion between two classes using Skype, blogs, and wikis.

A Bird's-Eye View of How to Build *Your* PLN

There are five initial practices that will be useful in building a PLN at any elementary, middle, or high school.

1. **Examine and evaluate availability of technology.** A clear understanding of the current status of the technology at your school is necessary before beginning to set up a PLN. As you design the technology survey for stakeholders (Resource A), it should only include realistic potential, and take into account the technology possibilities at your school site.

2. **Administer a needs assessment.** A needs assessment (Resource B) offers data from many perspectives and participants, from which unexpected results may emerge. It empowers all members of the school community and provides a space in which participants have a voice.

3. **Assemble a learning leadership team.** Based on the results of the technology survey, the needs assessment, and any additional data you have, put together a team that includes experts in each of the areas of weakness indicated in your data analyses. If not already indicated, include a technology expert, a curriculum specialist, and a representative from the administrative team of the school (preferably the principal).

4. **Use data to determine short- and long-term goals.** Once you've put together your learning leadership team, one of the first tasks that should be addressed is the gathering and analysis of all the teacher and student data you have available (Resource C). From this analysis, long- and short-term goals can be identified (Resource E).

5. **Communicate your goals with the entire school community.** In order for your goals to be accomplished, the entire school community needs to be aware of what the goals are and how they will be accomplished, and to have an action plan to achieve them.

REVIEW

Our hope is that, as a result of reading this book, each school community can successfully design and implement its own unique PLN that addresses its specific needs and increases student achievement. Based on the data available to us, we decided that our focus would include a blended use of technology that would support our schoolwide curriculum and professional development goals. Your areas of weakness may include discipline, attendance, morale, instruction, or others. Whatever areas you decide to focus on in your school community, a PLN can provide a framework from which members of your school community can

- Access information and resources
- Learn best instructional practices that would support your areas of focus
- Take leadership roles in addressing needs
- Communicate expectations and policies that align with goals and mandates
- Practice applying technology to daily instructional practice
- Collaborate with others to improve instructional strategies

 All of the resources described and presented in this book are also available at www.your professionallearningnetwork.com.

Resource A

Technology Survey

1. I would like to participate in professional development that focuses on technology tools in the classroom
   - ❑ Once per month
   - ❑ Once per quarter
   - ❑ Once per semester
   - ❑ Never

2. I would like to receive training on one or more of the following areas:
   - ❑ Website production
   - ❑ Handheld technology tools
   - ❑ Wikis/blogs
   - ❑ Web-based resources
   - ❑ PowerPoint
   - ❑ Keynote
   - ❑ Excel
   - ❑ Microsoft Word
   - ❑ Other: _____

3. I regularly use the following in my classroom as part of my instruction:
   - ❑ Teacher laptop (presentation/notes)
   - ❑ Student computers in the classroom
   - ❑ Computer labs
   - ❑ Document camera
   - ❑ Projector
   - ❑ Handheld technology tools
   - ❑ Interactive whiteboard
   - ❑ Other: _____

4. I would like to increase my use of the following as part of my classroom instruction:

 ❑ Teacher laptop (presentation/notes)
 ❑ Student computers in the classroom
 ❑ Computer labs
 ❑ Document camera
 ❑ Projector
 ❑ Handheld technology tools
 ❑ Interactive whiteboard
 ❑ Other: _____

5. I use technology (e-mails, wikis, blogs, websites) to collaborate with my colleagues at school:

 ❑ Daily
 ❑ Weekly
 ❑ Monthly
 ❑ Never

Resource B

Faculty Needs Assessment

1. Our goal at our school is always to increase student achievement. How do you define student achievement?

2. To which department and/or small learning community do you belong?

3. To which on-campus professional learning communities do you belong?

4. What type of professional development would you like to see offered at our school next year?

5. When attending a professional development session on campus, would you rather attend a face-to-face workshop or a web-based (online) workshop?
   ❑ Web-based
   ❑ Face-to-face

6. Would you be willing to take a short assessment after completing an online workshop in order to get points towards recertification?
   ❑ yes
   ❑ no

7. Which two statements best describe your struggling students' content area reading? Please select below:
   ❑ My students have difficulty with the textbook.
   ❑ Some do not understand how to navigate the textbook, while others do not understand the overall layout and relationship of the units, chapters, headings, and subheadings.
   ❑ My students simply look for the answers to questions. They don't read the text in its entirety, so they miss a lot of important information.
   ❑ My students read so slowly that they cannot keep up with the pace of the curriculum.
   ❑ My students try to read, but they have a lot of difficulty understanding the text and applying the concepts to their assignments and assessments.
   ❑ The content vocabulary is overwhelming for my students. They have difficulty remembering the meanings of words in the chapters and do not use them in conversations and writing.

8. Is there a literacy strategy that you would like to learn more about in order to enhance your teaching practices (using text structure, making connections, inference, finding the main idea and details, vocabulary, writing, other)?

9. What would you like to see added to our current forms of communication that would make communication more accessible or useful to you?

10. How can we make our current *methods* of communicating with the faculty better fit your needs?

11. Which of the following do you consider to be a needed area of improvement for our school?
   ☐ Student motivation
   ☐ Student discipline
   ☐ Faculty and staff communication
   ☐ Student engagement
   ☐ Master schedule
   ☐ Teacher motivation and morale
   ☐ Professional development opportunities on campus
   ☐ Professional development opportunities off campus
   ☐ Teacher use of technology
   ☐ Student use of technology
   ☐ Other _____

12. Do you have any suggestions to improve on the weaknesses identified in Question 11?

13. On average, how frequently do you participate in planning with other teachers, collaborating on lessons, observing peers, or modeling instructional practices for peers?
    - ❑ Daily
    - ❑ Twice per week
    - ❑ Once per week
    - ❑ Twice per month
    - ❑ Once per month
    - ❑ Once per quarter
    - ❑ Never

14. On a scale of 1 to 5, with 5 being the most positive, how would you rate the importance of a collegial atmosphere in our school community? (collaboration, planning, evaluating, and assessing together)

    1   2   3   4   5

15. If you believe that increased collegiality and collaboration is important for increasing student achievement schoolwide, what methods or strategies do you believe would be effective in achieving this goal?

Resource C

Data Analysis for Areas of Focus (worksheet)

Stakeholders	Focus Area	
	Online Component	Face-to-Face Component
Administrators		
Teachers		
Students		

Resource D

*Data Analysis for Areas of
Focus (sample worksheet)*

	Motivation	
	Online Component	Face-to-Face Component
Administrators **Motivate teachers**	____Provide support (templates, resources, forum, content lessons)	____Provide support (explicit instruction from and available time of curriculum specialist, technology expert, and content area liaisons)
	____Decrease teacher workload (content lessons shared, rubrics and assessments shared, forum to voice concerns and collaborate, outstanding student examples available to share, professional development resources)	____Decrease teacher workload (superfluous meetings and committees eliminated, increased time allotted for planning within and across contents)
	____Increase teacher performance (access to student data, professional development	____Increase teacher performance (access to explicit instruction in how to interpret student data, hard

	Motivation	
	Online Component	Face-to-Face Component
	resources, model lessons and student work samples, forum)	copies of student data provided upon request, professional development offered for small group instruction based on requests of stakeholders)
	_____Ensure availability of content-based information for new teachers and those who lack expertise (curriculum folders, sample lessons, model lessons, student samples, etc.)	_____Ensure availability of content-based information (curriculum notebooks, sample lessons, model lessons, student samples, etc.)
Teachers **Motivate students**	_____Provide models of student work to exemplify examples and nonexamples for assignments	_____Provide models of student work containing examples and nonexamples for assignments
	_____Opportunity for discussion of rubrics, assignments, etc., resulting from the contents of content folders	_____Opportunity for discussion of rubrics, assignments, etc., resulting from the implementation of new core curriculum and components associated with schoolwide goals

	Motivation	
	Online Component	Face-to-Face Component
	_____Establish common language and consistent instructional frame so that expectations are clear and achievement is more fluid across contents. (i.e., each class begins with a kickoff with common focus, such as text structure or questioning)	_____Establish common language and consistent instructional frame so that expectations are clear and achievement is more fluid across contents. (i.e., each class begins with a kickoff with common focus, such as text structure or questioning)
Students **Motivate themselves**	_____Stay up-to-date with assignments, even with absences	_____Stay up-to-date with assignments, even with absences
	_____Be able to spend more time on difficult concepts by reviewing and revisiting outside of the classroom	_____Be able to spend more time on difficult concepts by reviewing and revisiting outside of the classroom

Resource E

Long-Term Goals With Short-Term Steps (chart)

Long-term goal 1:	*Timeline*
Short-term goals to support long-term goal:	
Long-term goal 2:	
Short-term goals to support long-term goal:	
Long-term goal 3:	
Short-term goals to support long-term goal:	

Resource F

Long-Term Goals with Short-Term Steps (sample chart)

Long-term goal #1: **Design a professional learning network that addresses specific needs of our school community.**	*Timeline*
Short-term goals to support long-term goal: • Administer and analyze a needs assessment within the school community • Administer a survey to determine most appropriate environment/platform to house school's professional learning network • Determine nonnegotiable based on data • Develop common instructional frame based on data • Develop plan for the lowest quartile, including a mentoring program • Launch professional learning network and populate folders to support nonnegotiables and instructional frame	_____ _____ _____ _____ _____ _____
Long-term goal #2: **Familiarize teachers and administrators with an educational management system.**	
Short-term goals to support long-term goal: • Assemble a learning leadership team that includes experts in each of the areas of weakness indicated in data analyses of the needs assessment • Show administrators how to communicate in online environment, monitor teacher use of chosen platform, access and check lesson plans (a nonnegotiable), use and recommend professional development resources, etc. • Meet with small groups of teachers to introduce professional learning network, including: core curriculum folders, lesson plan submission instructions, forum, kickoffs, common instructional frame, and professional development resources	_____ _____ _____

CHAPTER 2

Zooming in on Leadership

I felt by being a content area liaison I was able to get informed about ManateeLearn and speak with other teachers to get their opinions and views. I felt I had an impact on positive changes at our school for both new and seasoned teachers. The format of ManateeLearn is very user friendly, so with the training that I received I was confident in approaching and discussing possible concerns with my fellow teachers. My department members were confident in me and felt comfortable coming to me to ask questions.

—Nikki Plummer, science teacher, content area liaison

WHY A LEADERSHIP FOCUS FOR A PLN?

Although the principal of a school is expected to be its instructional leader, a strong principal identifies expertise in potential future leaders and shares some responsibilities within the school community with them, thus empowering others and enlarging the possibilities for increased student growth and focus on achievement (Marzano, Waters, & McNulty, 2005). We developed a structure for leadership at our school site which has provided a pathway in guiding our processes for thinking about, designing, and implementing our PLN and its components. Consequently, it makes sense to begin the conversation with an examination and explanation of the leadership system that is in place at our school, as we feel it affected the choices and success of the components we chose to include as integral parts.

SNAPSHOT OF LEADERSHIP IN *OUR* PLN

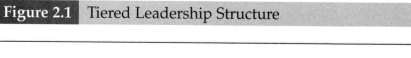

Figure 2.1   Tiered Leadership Structure

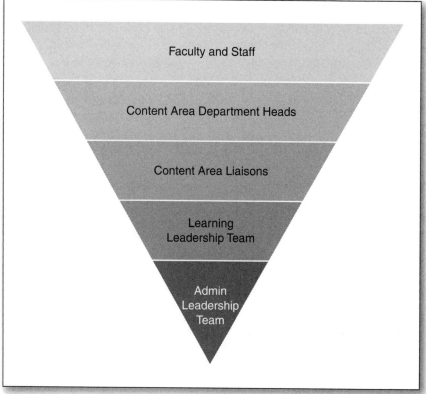

Tiered Leadership Structure

When we were in the beginning stages of trying to figure out how to best design our PLN, it became obvious that it would be a huge undertaking requiring much support and expertise. We decided that we needed to expand the current notion of leadership to include more stakeholders' voices and perspectives, empower additional teachers, lessen the burden on the administrative leadership team, and increase the expertise in building the PLN. We thus formalized our tiered leadership structure.

As illustrated in Figure 2.1, there are five tiers in our leadership structure. Our goal was the formation of an inclusive and unified community of educators and the expansion of the number of leaders. We have represented this in the figure by placing the broad base of the triangle at the top, with the highest-level leadership at the bottom. Below are the details that accompany the choices, composition, duties, and contributions of each of these leadership teams.

Administrative Leadership Team

Our school is a large high school with a principal and four assistant principals. Together, these administrators comprise the administrative leadership team. Each member of the administrative team has specified roles and responsibilities that include overseeing at least one content area department and its members; therefore, they each have a vested interest in the quality of instructional practices and the accompanying curriculum.

The administrative team conducts walkthroughs, which are in essence daily observations, of the classrooms for which they are responsible. They are looking for the use of specified instructional strategies that contribute toward the schoolwide goals. The curriculum, along with its accompanying instructional practices, is the responsibility of the entire administrative team, but each administrator is held accountable for specified departments.

Learning Leadership Team

In order to build in some accountability to the faculty for taking their needs seriously and addressing them appropriately, some sort of leadership team with expertise in data analysis, technology, and curriculum needs to be in place.

We called our group of experts the *Learning Leadership Team*. This title implies, first, that we are all leaders, and will act accordingly. Second, it implies that we are each lifetime learners, aware that we continue to have much to learn, regardless of our current levels of knowledge and education. Finally, it implies that we are a team, prepared to engage in deep discussions and consider issues from new perspectives, and willing to compromise with regard to our individual goals and to put aside personal agendas in order to move the school forward.

Our first order of business was to analyze our technology survey, needs assessment, and other data we had gathered. Our second order of business was to present the findings to the teachers and administrators, provide a space for feedback, and begin to form the framework for the components that would most accurately and immediately address our specific needs as a school community.

Because curriculum and technology play integral roles at any school site, we chose representatives from each of these areas to serve on the learning leadership team. These people will speak for their committees and for the faculty at large. An administrator is also an important part of this team because he or she is the head of the school, reports back to the administrative leadership team, and offers a necessary administrative perspective in the discussions and decisions that are made by the learning leadership team. In addition, this team has members who are knowledgeable about designated areas of weakness.

This team was instrumental in the design, building, and implementation of our network. Its members had to be able to get along well, to articulate thoughts, and to think outside the box.

Content Area Liaisons

Our content area liaisons are multitalented individuals; their role is as a necessary bridge between the top (or bottom, Figure 2.1) leadership teams and the faculty members. They are chosen based first on their ability to get along with others and their leadership potential. Their main duty is to act as liaisons between higher tiers of leadership—the administrators, the literacy leadership team, and technology committee—and their department members, so they must be people to whom their peers would be willing to learn from and go to for help.

We next consider their level of content knowledge, because they need to be able to speak with expertise in their subject areas in order to articulate needs and suggest improvements. It is helpful if they have some knowledge of technology, but willingness to learn may be acceptable.

Finally, and most importantly, they must be willing to serve the school community. It is a big responsibility to serve as a content area liaison, and our school currently does not have the budget to compensate them for the extra work that will be required of them. The goal is to have representatives from each content area, but it is better to start out with a small qualified group than to simply take what you can get. As the administrative leadership team hires new teachers in subsequent years, it can take into consideration whether or not interviewees would make strong candidates to serve in the future as content area liaisons.

At our school, one of the first requirements of the content area liaisons was to serve as models and teachers to their peers in demonstrating how to log on to ManateeLearn and navigate the site. Although not all of our content area liaisons are technology experts, they were each willing to go through an hour-long training session during the summer to learn how to log on, upload plans and documents, and make suggestions for additional uses. The benefits to our school community were substantial:

- We were able to determine whether or not our handouts, presentations, and other materials sufficed to explain the processes during our summer workshop. The liaisons offered valuable opinions and made contributions that strengthened our presentation to the faculty later.

- We had an additional 17 people who could help their peers with logging on and uploading lessons, presentations, documents, and other materials.
- We empowered them with a leadership role, giving them voices they may not have otherwise had in the decision-making processes of the school.
- This set the stage for them to be the first to be trained, to learn the features, and to participate in the activities on our network. They later became the first to participate in the forums; to upload lessons, presentations, and documents; and to scan in student work and upload it to the appropriate folders. They led the way as we navigated a lot of new territory.

Content Area Department Heads

Our department heads are considered the official instructional leaders at our school. They oversee the implementation of the curriculum, order necessary supplies, coordinate departmental goals, and facilitate department meetings. Because we were trying to expand the notion of leadership, we purposely chose not to have content area liaisons who were department heads. As such, the content area liaisons could report and model uses of the PLN during department meetings, but would not have the added responsibility of other duties. On the other hand, the department heads could retain their leadership roles within the department, but would be able to share the responsibility of learning how to access, navigate, and upload documents and information. This shared sense of responsibility increased the number of people who had ownership of the PLN but did not tax anyone's time and abilities unrealistically.

Faculty and Staff

This final tier of our leadership structure remains the most crucial, as it contains the largest number of members in our school community. In order for our PLN to evolve as a dynamic management system that serves our community's needs, we always need to be aware of the perceptions of the faculty and staff. We initially gained an overarching sense of needs and opinions based on our anonymous needs assessment and technology survey. We further learned about teachers' needs by opening forums in each of the content areas.

Establishing a tiered leadership schema and putting the teams into place prior to the design and implementation of our PLN gave us additional opinions and contributions from experts in many areas during the process of building our network. It also allowed the burden of responsibility to be shared among many capable professionals.

A Bird's-Eye View of Leadership for *Your* PLN

1. Examine your current leadership structure. We've included a tiered leadership graphic organizer (Resource G) for you to use as you consider your leadership teams and their roles in your school community.

2. Share the wealth. Provide opportunities for teachers to take leadership roles. Designing and implementing a PLN that addresses a school's needs takes a lot of work and requires expertise in many areas. Content area liaisons proved to be a valuable asset contributing to our success.

3. Add members to your learning leadership team based on areas of weakness. We recommend that each school site include members on its learning leadership team in the areas of weakness. For example, if your school has many opportunities for improvement in discipline, someone from the discipline committee should serve on the learning leadership team. If you do not already have a committee representing, researching, and learning about an area of weakness, the administrative leadership

team can form a committee whose purpose is to focus on that particular area. So, using discipline as an example, your school would form a discipline committee to examine and analyze your existing data on school discipline (such as tardy policy, referrals, and suspensions), delineate the major areas of weakness, learn about current plans that work at other similar schools, and develop a plan for growth and improvement at your school site. The discipline committee chairperson would also serve on the learning leadership team.

4. Know the strengths of your school community members. Some people's gifts include content area expertise. Other people are math wizards who can add columns of numbers in their heads. Still others get along well with everybody. The administrative leadership team should be aware of what strengths their teachers and staff members possess and ask them to serve in the capacities that would both empower them and work toward achieving the school's goals and objectives.

REVIEW

- Formalize your tiered leadership structure (Resource G). Fill in what leadership teams are going to be in place and the roles and responsibilities of each team. Communicate this clearly to all members of the school community.
- Once the leadership structure is in place, analyze data to determine weaknesses and delineate the school's focus.

 All of the resources described and presented in this book are also available at www.your professionallearningnetwork.com.

Resource G

Tiered Leadership Structure (graphic organizer)

Faculty and Staff

Content Area Department Heads

Content Area Liaisons

Learning Leadership Team

Admin Leadership Team

Content Area Dept. Heads
- ○ _____
- ○ _____
- ○ _____
- ○ _____
- ○ _____

Content Area Liaisons
- ○ _____
- ○ _____
- ○ _____
- ○ _____
- ○ _____

Learning Leadership Team
- ○ _____
- ○ _____
- ○ _____
- ○ _____
- ○ _____

CHAPTER 3

Going Digital

Infusing Technology Into a PLN

ManateeLearn is a one-stop place that all teachers can go to for information instead of searching many different websites on the Internet. Teachers can post their own lesson plans that can be shared by other teachers. As an administrator I can view their lesson plans directly online, which saves time. From a collaboration stand-point, the technology has helped teachers collaborate because it helps teachers meet any time they need to instead of only meeting face-to-face, which is not always possible in a large school environment.

—Matt Kane, Assistant Principal

WHY A TECHNOLOGY FOCUS FOR A PLN?

As more and more school leaders turn to technology for pro-fessional development and communication within their school sites, professional learning communities are being formed outside of school sites to fill a void in teacher collaboration. Educators are becoming self-starters, forming communities on their own through the use of Twitter, Facebook, Google, wikis, blogs, and websites to share information and resources with those in their field. In the meantime, schools are missing a valuable opportunity to provide their faculties with the resources and knowledge that they need to achieve common schoolwide goals. In addition, pockets of communities within the school site are working independently of one another instead of collaborating to achieve schoolwide goals. Schools must become leaders on the path to support teachers. Collaborative learning environments can provide the support to build powerful institutions of learning.

Chapter 1 provided the explanation of a PLN. By first identifying our schoolwide goals and outlining what we wanted to achieve, we were able to create a platform for "networked learning" (Stoll & Louis, 2007) for our staff. The wheels of education are always turning, and technology is developing more quickly than teachers can possibly keep up with; therefore, the need to establish a networked community that bound formerly independent functions of the school together to produce higher student achievement and foster greater morale among the staff was identified, and those needs were met through our PLN ManateeLearn.

In this chapter, we will first walk through our experience in combining a technology-based platform with existing face-to-face interactions to create a highly useful PLN. Our PLN collectively benefitted our school environment and acted as a springboard for teachers to dive further into the use of technology as a tool for learning.

After presenting a snapshot of our experience, we will provide the methods that can be used to incorporate technology into a PLN that will in turn help you to develop your own success story. Depending on the comfort zone of your team, and the overall expertise of your teachers, your PLN may start on Level 1 of the technology integration ladder and progressively move to Level 5 (Figure 3.1). As teachers advance in their use of technology in learning and communication, they will begin to adopt some of these technologies into their own lessons. We witnessed this process firsthand in the first year of our PLN. Wherever you begin, know that you are on the path that leads to many kinds of schoolwide improvements.

SNAPSHOT OF TECHNOLOGY ON *OUR* PLN

Being familiar with the concept of a professional learning community, we knew right away that we wanted to reach beyond some of the limitations of a PLC. While a PLC can take many different forms, the general definition of a PLC is a group that comes together with a common vision and common goals (Hord, 1997). With the new technologies available, much attention has been given to Web 2.0 and other tools to aid educators in developing *personal* learning networks to develop professionally as an individual. The concept of combining the advantages of personal learning networks and PLCs to create a *professional* learning network that supports the entire school is not new. What is new is that with the technology now available this network can become the one tool that will lead to the accomplishment of schoolwide goals. By utilizing the experience of the current staff, the availability of technologies already present, and the curriculum and standards that are to be taught, we linked the network and increased organization.

Figure 3.1 Path to Technology Integration

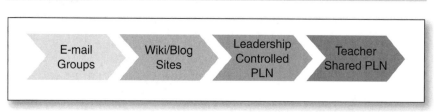

Before we began building the technology side of our PLN, we needed to review both the short-term and long-term goals. We started focusing on the first-year goals described in Chapter 1. Just as it is important to select the right technology tool to enhance classroom instruction, it was equally important to select the right tool for our PLN. After careful consideration of the skill level of our faculty, leadership team, and administrators, we chose to use the Moodle platform. There are other systems widely available that offer cost-efficient means with the same benefits. We will highlight these other tools later in this chapter.

The educational/course management system (EMS) Moodle was chosen because it allows for easy sharing of materials and resources, and, in a time of budget constraints, the cost of using Moodle through the use of the resources provided by the host website, Key to School, was minimal. In addition, Moodle was the platform adopted by the school district for student online courses. By continuing to use Moodle, our teachers benefit from gaining experience in using an increasingly popular EMS. For our purposes, we expanded the use of an EMS into a PLN, so from this point we will refer to the site as a PLN.

It is important to remember that, in addition to the asynchronous environment provided by our PLN, we also used face-to-face meetings to foster those who needed additional support in the area of training. While everyone initially attended the face-to-face meetings, the ease of using the PLN eventually provided staff members the choice of whether to use the online platform alone or to meet, both in person and online, to communicate in a blended manner.

Establishing the Entry Page of ManateeLearn

Through Moodle, the educational technology specialist has the ability to upload materials to each course. In our design, the entry page of http://www.manateelearn.com provided access to materials that supported the schoolwide goals mentioned in Chapter 1. These links included

- Tools for lesson plan development
- Links to access to student data
- Resources for a school writing plan
- Professional development links
- A school calendar
- Links to specific course resources
- Access to site-based small learning communities

Figure 3.2   Home Page of ManateeLearn (screenshot)

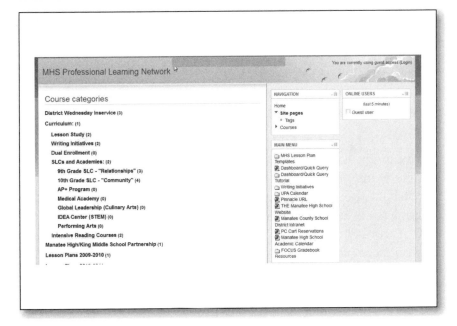

A BIRD'S-EYE VIEW OF TECHNOLOGY FOR *YOUR* PLN

Not every school site is going to have the resources or time to set up a PLN that uses the kind of technology that we incorporated. While using a method that allows for document sharing, forums for discussion, and storing of lesson plans is ideal, when this is not possible, steps can be taken that will eventually bring a school up to this level. The important part is to identify your organization's comfort level, and then with each success, reach towards the next level for continued school improvement.

In order to identify at what stage you should begin in developing a PLN, take some time to reflect on the following three key factors:

- The time you have to develop your PLN
- The technical expertise of your staff
- The equipment available at your school site

Using the planning guide presented in Resource H, you can determine where you should begin. While we want to always move forward, taking on too much in the beginning can lead to frustration and ultimately an inadequate PLN. After determining your level, proceed below to your personal starting point.

Stage 1: E-mail Groups

If your school is just beginning to adopt schoolwide goals, you might want to consider starting with Stage 1 of the technology integration plan. Stage 1 is ideal for schools where the teachers are perhaps not as technologically savvy and there is not a lot of time or money to implement the kind of training that would be required to get teachers to the point where they would be comfortable advancing their technology skills. E-mail is a tool that has already been introduced in practically every school site, and the majority of teachers know how to read their e-mails and respond appropriately.

In setting up a PLN via e-mail, the technology specialist should work with the administrator and curriculum coordinator to identify content area liaisons. A separate folder or icon should be set up within the e-mail system for each specified group. In some cases, e-mail groups may already be identified through departments. The content area liaisons will be responsible for communicating schoolwide goals to their particular group. In return, each group will set up personal goals for each of its members. These goals should help to realize the schoolwide goals. Content area liaisons should regularly e-mail their community to lead discussions about their progress toward their goals. Files and links to outside resources may also be shared in this manner. Some of the responsibilities of the content area liaisons for e-mail groups are

- To relay messages from the administration related to schoolwide improvements
- To inform the administration of the progress and concerns of their particular group
- To train all group members in how to send, receive, and reply to e-mails, as well as attach and download files and links

Some of the faculty nonnegotiables should include

- Participate regularly in e-mail discussions
- Keep the conversation positive
- Always offer suggestions that focus on improvement

Stage 2: Wiki/Blog Site

If your faculty has been participating in e-mail groups for some time, and you have not adequately met your schoolwide goals through this method, it is time to move on Stage 2: wikis or blogs. With websites such as PBWorks and Google, creating a log or wiki for collaboration has never been easier. The benefits of using a wiki or blog are numerous. They offer a more developed method of schoolwide collaboration. The PLN is always the sole focus of the site, so important communications do not get lost in the inbox. Teachers still have the ability to share files and to respond in groups; however, teachers also have the ability to respond to other groups when appropriate.

To begin your blog or wiki page, choose a host that is accessible within your school site. Due to different filters, it is usually best to stick to hosts that are designed to be used in the school environment. As mentioned above, both PBWorks and Google offer free services to educators, and are usually accessible at school sites. If you haven't checked out Google for Educators (http://www.google.com/educators/index .html), you are missing out on an array of free resources at your disposal. Both of these hosts are well-supported through their customer service options and would be an excellent starting point for a novice.

The responsibilities of the content area liaisons here are similar to the responsibilities of those in e-mail groups. Instead of the liaisons having more to do, the technology expert and the rest of the learning leadership team play a larger role in organizing the blog or wiki site to align with school goals. The responsibilities of the liaisons will still include

- Relaying messages from the administration related to schoolwide improvements through their group's blog or wiki page
- Informing the administration of the progress and concerns of their particular group by synchronizing communication and posting to the main page
- Training all group members in how to post and respond to a blog or wiki, as well as how to attach and download files and links

Some of the faculty nonnegotiables should include

- Participating regularly in blog discussions
- Keeping the conversation positive
- Always offering suggestions that focus on improvement

While a blog or wiki allows for better tracking and record keeping than an e-mail grouping system allows, it does have limits. When all the varying needs of a large school are incorporated into a blog or wiki that multiple groups are updating, the information can become overwhelming and convoluted. This is the reason for eventually escalating the technology tool your school is using to a tool, such as a web-based learning management, that is designed to improve organization system. However, for schools just beginning the process, a blog or wiki can provide enhanced communication among school staff.

Stage 3: Controlled PLN via a Management System

At the beginning of this chapter, we described our experience setting up our PLN. After surveying our resources, we determined that we would use a controlled learning management system (LMS) or educational management system (EMS). This is the system that is implemented at http://www.manateelearn.com. The word *controlled* indicates that the EMS is designed and maintained specifically and only by the technology and curriculum specialists. Input is received from the faculty, but the users of the site have limited privileges as to what files they can load into the site.

One of the major advantages of a controlled EMS to support a PLN is the organization that it provides. Specific links can be set up, ranging from schoolwide professional development to links that support one course. Within these links, a storage system similar to a file cabinet can be used to house resources that will be used in the current school year or in the following year. Files can be readily accessed and shared. Forums are also available for teachers to share their successes and offer ideas for other educators to incorporate into their teaching.

Once teachers are familiar with the platform and have an understanding of how to load material onto the site, then more control can be given to them, establishing a more teacher-led system. Through the controlled EMS, teachers can still collaborate and share files through the forum. The instructional technology specialist or the curriculum specialist still takes the primary role in adding other materials to the site.

Stage 4: Teacher-Led PLN via a Management System

The last of the four stages in developing a PLN is the teacher-led PLN. At this stage, all stakeholders are experienced in using the chosen platform and are confident in their ability to navigate through the site. Teachers are authorized to upload materials as they see fit. They are able to edit anything on the site, and have almost the same privileges on the site as does the instructional technology specialist. Due to the increased access by the staff, certain rules regarding organization of the site should be communicated and agreed upon to maintain that organization. For most organizations, a teacher-led PLN would be an aspiration that unfolds after many years of a controlled PLN.

REVIEW

Now that you have determined what platform is best for your environment, it is time to learn how to begin the process of designing your PLN. During this process, it is important to remember the following:

- Successful implementation can only occur when a realistic timeline is set and expectations are tied to goals and objectives.
- All stakeholders need to feel a sense of ownership in the process in order for the change to be embraced.
- By examining the checklist of topics and using your schools' needs and student data to narrow your focus, you can successfully navigate the steps to building your directed PLN.

All of the resources described and presented in this book are also available at www.your professionallearningnetwork.com.

Resource H

Technology Integration Matrix

Four Stages of Technology Integration	Stage 1: E-mail Groups	Stage 2: Wiki/ Blog Site	Stage 3: Controlled PLN	Stage 4: Teacher-Led PLN
Weekly Time Commitment for Leadership Team (after initial set-up)	Limited	1 to 2 hours	2 to 4 hours	2 to 4 hours
Equipment Requirement	Computers, Internet	Computers, Internet	Computers, Internet	Computers, Internet
Ability to Share Files in Groups	Yes	Yes	Yes	Yes
Ability to Create Forums	No	No	Yes	Yes
Easily Organize Information for Future Reference	No	No	Yes	Yes

CHAPTER 4

Landscape for Communication of Information

I believe that teachers were willing to buy into the mentoring program because the students' data were right there on ManateeLearn. Easy to find. If they have that data, then right then and there they can go ahead and get a strategy or resource that will help the students. Incorporate it into their instruction. That is the idea. Identify students in your classroom. Understand weaknesses looking at data. Commit to those students one-on-one to help move them toward achievement, graduation, and postsecondary success. I believe that our teachers were ready to move our students forward when they saw how many students were on the spreadsheet on ManateeLearn. They were willing to sign up to mentor them. Right then.

—Gary Theiler, Exceptional Student Education
teacher, mentor to six of our students, all of whom
showed growth in reading achievement

Why a Communication Focus for a PLN?

Our high school employs more than 100 people, so creating and using a reliable means of communication is quite difficult; it is important nonetheless. Our PLN is used as a hub for communication at our school. We have numerous components built into ManateeLearn that lend themselves to increased communication of information. We have organized our PLN so that it is easy to locate information, based on our school-wide goals and objectives.

A PLN is not a static entity, but one that is constantly emerging and changing as the needs of the school shift and change. We have reorganized several of our links and folders based on teachers' needs and requests. We plan to continue to review and revise it in order to increase the accessibility of information to the teachers and staff.

Snapshot of Communication on *Our* PLN

We will detail the choices we made to introduce our PLN as our platform for communication.

Schoolwide Goals and Objectives

Our schoolwide goals and objectives can be easily communicated and detailed on our PLN. All pieces of information can be discussed, posted, and reviewed there on a regular basis.

Our PLN has provided a platform for communication from which we have provided information both online and face-to-face. An example was seen in the common board configuration we adopted schoolwide this year. The expectation was for teachers to write or project the date, kickoff activity, essential questions and assessment each day. It was first introduced during a face-to-face faculty meeting. We then posted digital pictures of examples and nonexamples of the common board configuration, uploaded the PowerPoint presentation with definitions of each component of the configuration (including the purpose for each and why we chose to focus on these particular pieces), and provided data from the administrative classroom walk-throughs that show how our faculty members use the common board configuration. All this information is housed on our PLN site, so that teachers can easily access and review it at the point of need.

Feedback

Because submission of electronic lesson plans was a nonnegotiable and the submission of plans is a reason that all faculty members log on to our PLN regularly, the administrative leadership team decided that immediate and productive feedback on the lesson plans was necessary. We set up our network so that the lesson plans went automatically to the administrator who supervises that particular content area. Likewise, we set up our PLN so that feedback would be sent directly back to the teachers electronically, assuring the teachers that their lesson plans are being carefully considered. Our PLN provides a platform for ongoing conversations between the teacher and the administrator about professional growth, specific instructional strategies, kick-off topics, daily assessments, and other matters of concern. This has proven to be a quick and easy means for the administrative team to converse with the teachers about a variety of topics.

Calendar

We set up an interactive calendar to be accessed by all members of our school community. Because we have many interruptions to daily instruction (such as mandatory assessments, pep rallies, and fire drills) we decided we needed a central location to post all this information. As the teachers make their instructional plans, they can log in to ManateeLearn, examine the calendar, and make note of the upcoming events that may affect their teaching. The calendar also enables the teachers to schedule afterschool tutoring and parent meetings without having to worry about unexpected conflicts.

Initially, only the administrative leadership team could post activities and events on the calendar. Our goal is eventually to open it up to more stakeholders. We continue to revise and perfect its uses for our purposes so that it will remain a valuable part of our PLN in communicating information about schoolwide assessments, homerooms, fire drills, faculty meetings, and other matters.

Meetings and Presentations

Because we have a large population of teachers and staff who are involved in numerous clubs and activities, there are always some who are unable to attend our face-to-face faculty meetings, small learning community meetings, Response to Intervention team meetings, and other meetings. Our PLN enables every member of our school community (faculty, staff, and administrators) to access documents, presentations, and resources from each meeting that takes place on campus. Figure 4.1 shows an example of the postings resulting from our December faculty meeting.

Having this information available permits all faculty members to remain informed community members. It also removes the burden of distributing documents and discussing presentations with those who may have missed an important meeting. Often our school's face-to-face meetings include directives and explanations of district and state mandates and our school's focus and goals, so by posting all the information, not only can it be accessed by those who missed the meetings, but all resources and presentations can be reviewed, revisited, and accessed by each person at the point of need. We have found that teachers access many of the presentations after the meetings. Posting information in an asynchronous environment is a good way of differentiating for the many levels of knowledge in our school community. For those who are familiar with certain pieces of information, they are not required to revisit it; but for those for whom it may be a whole new concept, they have the opportunity to access it at their convenience and as the need may arise.

Figure 4.1	Faculty Meeting Handouts and Presentations (screenshot)

6

December: Differentiated Instruction with Focus on Differentiating by Using Engaging Daily Assessments

What is Differentiated Instruction
District's complete presentation on Differentiated Instruction
District's Participant Guide
MHS's Differentiated Presentation
*Melding Formative Assessment and Engagement
*Great ideas for Engaging Students Using Daily Assessments
10 Instructional Strategies to Engage while Assessing
Presentation with Explanations + Examples for 10 Instructional Strategies
Presentations for Engagement and Assessment with Differentiation from HSTW
MHS presentation
Some Indicators that You are Differentiating
Lacey Ryan's Wheel of Fortune Power Point (all contents)
Violeta Velazquez's Exit Slip
Joanne Whitley's presentation (math)
Summary of Classroom Observations
Informal Assessments (district)

This year, after the face-to-face meetings, teachers have been offering additional resources and documents. We post each of them on our PLN with the teacher's name in the link so that any faculty member who has a question about the information posted can go directly to the teacher and have a professional conversation, ask questions, and learn more. Figure 4.2 shows an example from our PLN that resulted from our faculty meeting with the focus on word analysis. Several of our teachers found the ideas embedded in the Frayer Model, word webs, and concept maps helpful, but wanted to adapt them for their own students' needs. As they came up with their own ideas, we posted their examples.

Without a PLN, these data would not have been available in one space for all to access at any time. Although it would have been possible to communicate all this information through e-mails with attachments, it would have taken up a lot of space, it might have been difficult to find later, or might have gotten lost among the many pieces of information that teachers receive. As a part of our PLN, all the information is available if you want or need it, but it is not required that everyone access everything posted.

Student Data

Because our PLN is secure and accessed by known participants who have been given a user name and password, we are also able to share student data within our school community. Last year, the student population that showed the smallest gain in reading achievement was our lowest 25th percentile. We initiated a mentoring program in which teachers could volunteer to mentor a student in this lowest quartile. We were able to post the requirements and expectations for our mentors and provide a link to an interactive spreadsheet that contained the students' data. We created a column on the spreadsheet on which teachers could sign

| Figure 4.2 | Faculty Members Contribute to ManateeLearn (screenshot) |

3
October/November Resources: Word Analysis

- District Power Point: Word Analysis
- Frayer Model for Vocabulary
- English: Jon Scott's Frayer Model
- Vocational: Laura Sollenberger's frayer model
- Concept Map (Broad Overview)
- Word Web (similar word parts)
- Social Studies: Colby West's presentation (word web + 2-column notes)
- Academic Vocabulary Lists (alphabetical)
- Academic Word List (frequency)
- Academic Word List (sublists in order of frequency)
- word map alternative
- word walls at MHS
- Prefixes and Suffixes (verbs and nouns)
- most common prefixes and suffixes
- Greek and Latin Root Words
- Spelling Tests for 100 Words Every High School Graduate Should Know

next to the students' names to be their mentors. We could all view the interactive spreadsheet, so that if a student was having difficulty in a class, the teacher could click on a link and find the child's mentor in order to talk with that mentor about the student's areas of difficulty. The spreadsheet is also updated at regular intervals to include progress monitoring assessments, so that mentors and teachers can check for growth in achievement.

There are numerous sites that all the members of our school community visit on a regular basis: a site to access our electronic grade book; a database that houses student data, including students' schedules, discipline referrals, absences, assessment scores, and other information; an Intranet for our district; our school website; and others. All teachers have access to data via the World Wide Web and databases, but it is sometimes hard to remember where to find which student data. On our PLN, we have links for each of these sites on our main menu. Teachers can simply log on to ManateeLearn and click on whatever links they may need. We know this is a useful part of our PLN because the link for the database has been used 556 times, while the link to the electronic grade book has been accessed 2,370 times thus far this year.

Figure 4.3	Main Menu Featuring Links to Student Data (screenshot)

Trends and Mandates

We also use the PLN site to communicate information and resources with regard to changes in education. Our state has just made some changes in the content and formatting of our high-stakes testing, so as we gather information and learn about dates and deadlines, we post memos from the state department of education, links to the latest updates, and other pertinent information for all teachers to access at any time. Our goal is to keep teachers informed and ensure familiarity with important initiatives and programs that may eventually become mandated for the classroom.

Education will never be static. There are always new ideas, initiatives, and requirements that originate at the district, state, or federal level. Regardless of the topic or initiative, the PLN is a useful platform from which to communicate information to the members of our network community.

A BIRD'S-EYE VIEW OF COMMUNICATION ON *YOUR* PLN

Each of the links and folders on our PLN can be used with all grade levels. Each school, whether elementary, middle, or secondary, can benefit from a schoolwide hub of communication such as a PLN provides. Every school needs to be able to clearly articulate goals and objectives to its stakeholders. Administrators and leadership teams need a means by which to provide productive feedback to teachers in a variety of situations, kindergarten through 12th grade. The key to developing an effective communication model is to keep in mind that communication is most productive when community members take ownership by accessing and reviewing the information communicated, engage in meaningful dialogues and conversations about the information, and apply the information communicated to classroom instruction so as to increase student achievement. In order to tailor your model for communication to the needs at your school, follow the steps below:

1. Determine current weaknesses in communication.

2. Prioritize information communicated. In our world today, we have information overload. Design the PLN

for your school community as you would create your own *personal* learning network: put the most important information and links on the entry page or on the main menu. Eliminate unnecessary links, folders, and outlier tidbits. A PLN is a platform for communicating important professional information. School community members must be able to distinguish between what is most and least important. Your schoolwide goals and objectives take priority.

3. Offer multiple opportunities for deep understanding of prioritized information. If the information communicated is important, threads to enhance understanding can be provided on your PLN. For example, you can post an expectation for the use of research-based instructional strategies on the entry page. Additionally, this expectation can be embedded in the curriculum components of your PLN, a professional development module can be created, a discussion thread can be set up, and handouts from faculty meetings can be uploaded. Important information can be posted, explained, and reviewed, keeping in mind that multiple meaningful exposures increase the probability of understanding and use.

4. Provide feedback. Productive feedback can lead to increased understanding, improved practice, and engagement in professional dialogues and conversations. It must be specific and timely. A PLN can be used as a platform from which to provide feedback to teachers about lesson plans, observations, committee work, and other areas.

REVIEW

The following key points from this chapter are applicable to teachers and students at all grade levels.

- Organize and prioritize information on your PLN.

  Information that is easy to find and use can be accessed quickly at the point of need. Teachers do not typically have time to waste searching for information. A user-friendly PLN is the goal.

- Engage in two-way communication.

  Dialogues between PLCs, small learning communities, departments, and administrators about schoolwide goals and objectives can lead to deeper professional conversations, a more informed community, and a broader understanding of the information being disseminated.

- Be inclusive.

  It is sometimes difficult to include each person in every announcement, invitation, committee, and small learning community in a school setting. A PLN provides a platform in which any teacher can partake in professional development, read handouts from meetings, access lessons and presentations, or examine and analyze student data. As communication is increased and exclusivity is eliminated, a school community can become more cohesive.

- Go green.

  A PLN will prove to be a greener means of communication, as it will no longer be necessary to make hard copies of documents during professional development sessions or face-to-face faculty meetings.

CHAPTER 5

Framing Curriculum and Instruction

Being able to access my old lesson plans through ManateeLearn has been helpful, especially as a new teacher, because I'm able to improve on what I did last year and revisit assessments I used that worked. I also like getting feedback from the administrators.

—Erica Weiffenbach, second-year teacher

WHY A CURRICULUM FOCUS FOR A PLN?

The discussion of designing a PLN at our school began around the subject of curriculum. The adoption and implementation of a recently purchased common core curriculum was going to affect teachers in a variety of ways. Some teachers felt insulted because they would no longer be able to teach specific units that they and their students had always enjoyed, while other teachers were relieved to finally have a guideline that explicitly stated expectations and provided a pacing guide.

Based on teachers' reactions, the administrative leadership team began to question how this new curriculum was going to affect our school community. When they considered options for how they could support the teachers, possibilities of some sort of an EMS started to emerge as a practical solution. As we began to design the early conceptions of a PLN, some of the main pieces were originally targeted to increase focus on instruction, encourage collaboration, and boost motivation; in the process, we kept in mind that our ultimate goal was to raise student achievement.

The learning leadership team began our brainstorming sessions during the spring and summer prior to the launching of our network in the fall. The content of our early conversations was almost exclusively about two changes our teachers were going to encounter in the fall: lesson plan requirements and core curriculum implementation.

SNAPSHOT OF CURRICULUM ON *OUR* PLN

In-depth discussions based on these new requirements, our teachers' needs, and our students' data resulted in the development of a common instructional model that would support our teachers' uses of best instructional practices while addressing our students' academic needs. This model dictated what the lesson plan templates would include, highlighted schoolwide curricular goals, and was housed on our PLN in the curriculum folder for each subject area. Each aspect of the common instructional model is supported by researched-based best practices and has been shown to lead to increased student achievement (Westerberg, 2009; Marzano, Waters, & McNulty, 2005). The common instructional model ensures that we

- Explicitly teach strategies that address our schoolwide academic weaknesses
- Use research-based best instructional practices in our teaching methods

- Monitor progress with the use of informal daily assessments
- Document the use of interventions and chart the resulting student growth

Common Instructional Model

Figure 5.1 Common Instructional Model (screenshot)

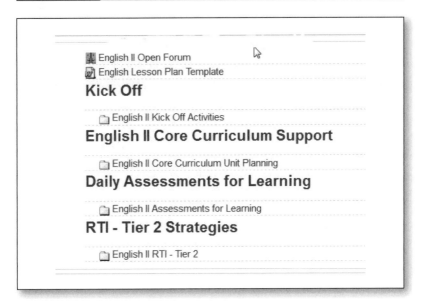

An example of the common instructional model for English II can be seen in Figure 5.1. Each subject area's common instructional frame includes

- An open forum link
- A lesson plan template link
- A kickoff folder
- A core curriculum support folder
- A folder for daily assessments for learning
- A Response to Intervention (RTI) Tier 2 strategies folder

Below is a description of the contents of each these links and folders and a detailed explanation of how the teachers access and use them in order to increase their students' achievement.

Open Forum Link

Our forums were initially designed and used to give a voice to teachers with regard to issues specific to the mandated core curriculum. Teachers might post when they were having difficulties with the pacing or with a particular unit performance assessment (UPA), or they might offer advice to others who were teaching the same content, perhaps to help them avoid a particular problem. An early example that was posted on our world history forum follows:

Figure 5.2   Open Forum for World History (screenshot)

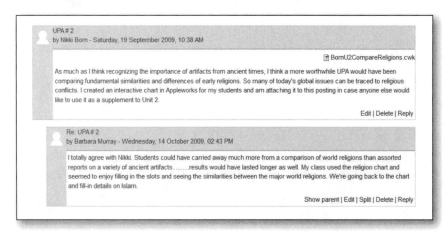

As is evident in Figure 5.2, Ms. Born created a graphic organizer as a solution to her frustration with a missed opportunity in the focus of the lesson provided by the core curriculum. Ms. Murray, another world history teacher, read the post, used Ms. Born's resource, and attested that her students benefitted from using the graphic organizer. This type of interaction was quick, collaborative, and could lead to increased student achievement.

Because there can sometimes be a tendency to quickly become negative when given a space to post complaints, we added a requirement that ensured posts would be productive and end on a positive note like the example above. All members of our school community were required to adhere to the following format when posting on the forums:

1. Describe the concern with specificity.

2. Suggest a possible solution.

Below is an example of a discussion thread from the Algebra I forum. It demonstrates a specific concern with a plan of action to solve the problem. As can be seen in his reply, the district curriculum specialist corrected the problem within a day of the posting. Also evidenced is the willingness of the math teachers to share the responsibility and the positive effects of their collaboration. This quick interaction led to an exam that was more appropriate in that it would now provide the correct answer choices and better graphs, thereby saving the students and teachers unnecessary frustrations when taking and grading the exam.

Figure 5.3   Open Forum for Math (screenshot)

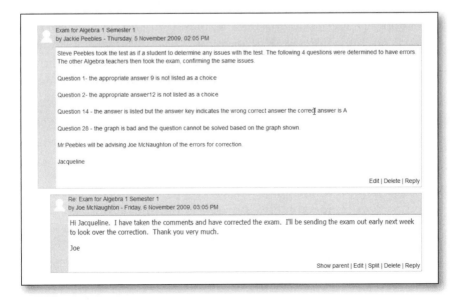

Providing teachers with access to a forum can give them a voice in the decision-making processes at a school, increase collaboration, and lead to increased student achievement with the use of more targeted lessons and assessments. The forums also provided us with a permanent record of problems and concerns. Teachers have a multitude of daily duties and responsibilities, so they may not remember specific frustrations and problems with individual lessons from one year to the next. Documentation of problems as they arise serves as a reminder and ensures that they will be addressed during the midyear and end-of-year reviews by the school and the district.

Lesson Plan Template Link

Our district provided general guidelines for the newly mandated lesson plans but did not require a specific format. The goal was therefore to give the guidelines to departments and have each department collaboratively create a lesson plan template which would address the specific needs of that particular content area. These newly created templates were then uploaded into the folder for that content area.

The administrative leadership team met several times and discussed how to best manage the lesson plans that would be turned in every two weeks by over 100 faculty members. It would be a lot of paper to handle, read through, provide feedback on, and monitor. The learning leadership team and the administrative leadership team collaborated (discussed, brainstormed, compromised, and revised) about possibilities. They decided that electronic submission of lesson plans would be mandatory for the entire faculty. The main reasons behind this decision were

- Ease: It would (eventually) be easier for teachers to complete and submit lesson plans electronically, and it would (eventually) be easier for the administrative team to organize, give feedback, and monitor the lesson plans electronically with the help of an EMS.

- Archival access: The teachers always have access to their lesson plans, regardless of which computer they use or when they uploaded them.
- Regular log-on: Our goal was for our PLN to become the "go-to" place from which members of the school community would access their electronic grade books and attendance records, examine student data, participate in professional development, and use curriculum folders to get lesson presentations, student samples of work, and other materials. Regular log-on to upload plans fostered teachers' use of the PLN and provided a natural migration toward the technological component of the PLN. Even the most technology-reluctant teachers were able to take part by uploading and sharing lesson plans.
- Increase technology use and level: Many of our teachers had no prior experience with an EMS. The hope was to get them comfortable enough with navigating the system to want to implement a similar system with their students in their classrooms, so that instructional practices could be updated and more closely address the students' needs with the use of technology.

Kickoffs

Kickoffs at our school are the first order of business in every classroom, every period. They consist of a 3- to 7-minute minilesson that focuses on weaknesses reflected in our students' achievement data. Initially, these kickoffs were school-wide. At the beginning of last year, all content areas focused on text structures because the data indicated a weakness in that area. Then, at the first department meetings, teachers in each content area studied the data from that area and chose a specific structure on which to focus within that particular subject. For example, our social studies department chose to focus their kickoff lessons on cause-effect patterns and temporal sequences; the science department chose problems and solutions. For teachers who did not have expertise in text structures, many resources were posted under our professional development section on our PLN, by department, to provide additional classroom examples, graphic organizers, professional articles, and other materials. The resources were available to all, but no requirements were made for accessing the resources.

This year, our focus has been on the use of high-level words to move our students toward more critical thinking activities. Each department is in the process of choosing how they are going to highlight the increased use of high-level words, investigating best teaching practices with regard to vocabulary, word analysis, the uses of word walls, and using cooperative learning to increase critical thinking by the students. Multiple resources have been posted on our PLN.

Kickoffs have led to increased use of bell-to-bell instruction, indicated in our walkthrough observation data. Students know to look for the kickoff as soon as they enter the classroom at the beginning of each period. They hear and use common language, apply the same strategies to different contents, and have ample practice throughout each day. These kickoffs have also led to increased collaboration by the teachers because they have provided teachers across and within content areas with a common focus. The math department worked last summer to develop kickoffs based on their student data. Each teacher has a thick notebook of potential daily kickoffs that are applicable to student needs. The English department is planning to work together this summer to develop common grade-level kickoffs that address their students' needs for next year.

Core Curriculum Support Folders

When teachers click on the core curriculum unit planning link, core curriculum folders for each unit appear. For example, in biology the folders are labeled: Unit 1 Biology, Unit 2 Biology, etc. Each of these folders contains two folders, entitled *Resources* and *UPA*.

Figure 5.4	Curriculum Folders: Physical Science Resources (screenshot)

Physical Science Core Curriculum Unit Planning

```
P.S._Core_Curriculum_Units
   P.S._Unit_1
      Resources
         NatureofScience.ppt
         PS_Ch._2_Matter.ppt
      UPA
         plummer_phys_science_unit_1_handout_rubric.pdf
         plummer_unit_1_UPA_example_1.pdf
         plummer_unit_1_UPA_example_2.pdf
         plummer_unit_1_UPA_example_3.pdf
         plummer_unit_1_UPA_example_4.pdf
         scan0002.pdf
         Unit_1_UPA.doc
   P.S._Unit_2
      Resources
         PS_Ch._3_Part_1.ppt
         PS_Ch._3_Part_2.ppt
         PS_Ch._4_Part_1_Atomic_Structure.ppt
         PS_Ch._4_Part_2_Element_Families.ppt
      UPA
         Unit_2_UPA.doc
   P.S._Unit_3
      Resources
         PS_Ch.8_Acid_Base.ppt
         PS_Ch._5_Compounds.ppt
      UPA
```

Resources

Figure 5.4 shows an example of a *Resources* folder for Unit 2 in physical science. This folder is used by teachers to upload presentations, activities, materials, and resources for their particular lessons in their classrooms. During the first year of our

| Figure 5.5 | Curriculum Folders: English II UPAs (screenshot) |

English II Core Curriculum Unit Planning

```
⊟ Unit_1
    Resources
  ⊟ Unit_Performance_Assessment
    ⊟ Unit_1_UPA
         English_2_UPA_Unit_1_example_2.pdf
         English_2_UPA_Unit_1_example_3.pdf
         English_II_UPA_Unit_1_Example_1.pdf
       English_II_UPA_Unit_1_Example_1.pdf
       Myth_Partner_Project.docx
       Storybook_Myth_Rubric.docx
⊟ Unit_2
  ⊟ Resources
       In_the_Time_of_the_Butterflies.ppt
  ⊟ Unit_Performance_Assessment
       Eng_II_UPA_Sample_1.doc
       Eng_II_UPA_Sample_2.doc
⊟ Unit_3
  ⊟ Resources
       EnglishIIUnit3KeyConcepts.docx
       English_II_Honors_Unit_3_Essential_Question.docx
       English_II_Honors_Unit_3_vocabulary.docx
       English_II_Honors_Unit_3_vocanswers.docx
       rubricforblog.doc
       WRITING_RUBRIC.docx
```

PLN, the teachers uploaded the presentations as they created them. This year, they are able to access everything already in the folders and to add to the folders' existing contents. For example, all physical science teachers have access to everything in the physical science folders. They are invited to use any of those activities or presentations in their teaching practices.

UPA

Figure 5.5 shows an example of a *UPA* folder for English II. This folder contains student samples of Unit Performance

Assessments (UPA), or end-of-unit assessments. The content area liaisons or teachers scan and upload exemplars of student work for each unit. These examples can be shared with students in subsequent years to demonstrate how to interpret rubrics, to convey expectations, and to provide examples of excellence. The teachers now have permanent examples of student work that they can project, share, demonstrate, and use as models with their students as they are setting expectations, discussing projects, explaining rubrics, and grading assessments.

Visual aids can scaffold students in their understanding of expectations, so our hope is that these examples will lead to better understanding and increased levels of achievement. As we increase the rigor in our classrooms, we can continue to upload student samples of excellence for each unit's expectations. These samples can be used by all teachers in a particular subject area.

Daily Assessments for Learning and RTI Tier 2

As part of our common instructional model, we included folders entitled *Daily Assessments for Learning* and *RTI Tier 2* for each subject area. Although these folders were posted and goals for populating them were in place, they were part of our long-range plans, and they remained virtually untouched during our first year. We included them in our common instructional model because we wanted to familiarize stakeholders with goals for populating them in the future, to educate teachers on what daily assessments might look like, and to introduce the faculty to the components of Response to Intervention. A valuable lesson we learned our first year was to focus on a few things and do them well, rather than trying to put everything into place all at once.

The concept of a PLN was new for many faculty members, and some found its complexity challenging. Learning how to use a digital template to write lesson plans and then to upload the plans was a big task. Some of the goals for the first year included implementing a core curriculum and uploading presentations, lessons, and activities. Our second-year goals for the curriculum component of our PLN included populating the *Daily Assessments for Learning* and *RTI Tier 2* folders.

This year, the second year of implementation, we have specific expectations for implementing daily assessments of learning in each classroom. For teachers who are unfamiliar with assessing students' learning on a daily basis, we offered an online professional development module on our PLN.

In addition, we are formalizing our Response to Intervention framework and expectations this year. We have posted additional resources for RTI in the professional development section. As teachers start to document Tier 2 interventions and graph students' growth, we will begin to populate the RTI Tier 2 folders.

A BIRD'S-EYE VIEW OF CURRICULUM ON *YOUR* PLN

Each of the curricular components found on our PLN can be used with all grade levels. Each school, whether elementary or secondary, has schoolwide curriculum goals and expectations. Every school has curricular components that include lessons, activities, presentations, assessments, and progress monitoring. The key to developing an effective instructional model is to keep in mind best instructional practices that have been shown to increase student achievement. Every aspect of our PLN's common instructional model supports teacher and student needs at our school. In order to tailor your instructional model to the needs at your school, follow the steps below:

1. Determine your curricular focus. You may set up the folders on your PLN in any way that works for your own school community. We have provided a chart to help you figure out what components it makes the most sense to include in your instructional model based on your specific data and needs (Resource I). Determining a schoolwide focus for instruction enabled us to share across subjects and to access like-subject information and resources within subjects.

2. Consider how mandates can fit into your plan. Your school community may have different mandates dictated

by federal, state, or district leaders, but your PLN can address and incorporate any directive into its framework. As mandates come along, we can include them into our overarching plans and communicate their components through the curriculum expectation and professional development components of our PLN. For example, in our case, RTI is a directive that we have to incorporate into our curricular instructional practices, but your school community may have some other requirement. Whatever the requirements and expectations are at your school, you can expand your teachers' knowledge about them and put into place pieces that increase the use of specific practices as part of your curricular folders.

3. Connect your curricular goals to your short- and long-term goals. Once you have determined your focus and goals for instruction, review the short- and long-term goals developed earlier. Be sure to connect your curricular goals to your schoolwide short- and long-term goals. If your goals don't have a common focus, they may lose credibility. Look for common threads, patterns, and trends and connect them on your PLN.

4. Develop your instructional framework. We have provided a planning sheet that will help you set specific goals and determine the steps necessary to achieve these goals once you have decided what the components of your instructional model will be. This blank template includes a midyear review and a year-end review that can be used to monitor progress toward your goals. (Resource J). We have also included the planning sheet we used for our school to serve as an example of how you might use the worksheet (Resource K).

REVIEW

Although our primary curricular goal is increased student achievement, secondary benefits from the common instructional model on our PLN include professional discussions that have affected pedagogy and increased collaboration between learning communities, teams, and teachers. Key points from this chapter that are applicable to teachers and students at all grade levels include:

- A common instructional model can provide a framework toward increased student achievement if the focus requires the use of research-based best instructional practices.
- Kickoffs can increase the time spent on task. The students learn to look for the kickoff as soon as they enter the classroom and focus on academic goals immediately.
- Teachers' use of a common language (*text structures, text features, signal words, scanning, skimming*, etc.) ensures that students will hear the same words used multiple times a day in a variety of contexts. This frequent and repeated exposure to the same vocabulary across contents will enable students to begin to recognize, understand, and use the words appropriately in their speech and writing.
- Collaboration builds a sense of community while decreasing an individual teacher's workload. It is a productive form of cooperative learning.
- Scaffolding students by using an exemplar as a visual model of expectations can increase understanding of assignments, expectations, and assessments. Increased understanding can lead to increased achievement.
- Using informal daily assessments that are engaging will enable teachers to quickly identify areas of weakness for the students, differentiate based on student need, and align instruction with students' current levels of knowledge.

All of the resources described and presented in this book are also available at www.your professionallearningnetwork.com.

Resource I

Common Instructional Model: What Is Your Focus?

	Areas That Need Attention in the Classroom	Resulting Schoolwide Goals and Objectives	Instructional Strategies to Achieve Goals	Progress Monitoring Tools
Data Analysis				
Mandates				
Short- and Long-Term Goals				
Resulting Professional Development				

Resource J

Common Instructional Model (blank template)

Common Instructional Model Components	Goals for First Semester	Midyear Review	Year-End Review

Resource K

Common Instructional Model (sample)

Common Instructional Model Components	Goals for First Semester	Midyear Review With Modified Goals Based on Data	Year-End Review
Kickoffs	Schoolwide Focus on Vocabulary * Word walls *Provide content vocabulary definitions to students *Introduce Greek and Latin roots, prefixes, suffixes, etc. *Word maps, Frayer Model, graphic organizers	Use Progress Monitoring to determine increase in: *explicit teaching of words (walkthrough data) *students' word knowledge (classroom dialogue, writing) Walkthrough data on use of word walls and kickoffs	
Curriculum / Lessons	*Increase focus on teacher uploads into resource folders *Increase use of folders on ManateeLearn.com	*Focus on quality of student samples in folders. Compare to last year's student exemplars to note better word choices and improved student products.	
Daily Assessments	*Professional development on: 1. word analysis strategies 2. common board configuration 3. daily assessment possibilities *Begin accountability process for daily assessments	*Use walkthrough data and common board configurations to note needs with daily assessments. *Survey faculty for change in student achievement resulting from daily informal assessments.	

Common Instructional Model Components	Goals for First Semester	Midyear Review With Modified Goals Based on Data	Year-End Review
Interventions	Begin implementation of RTI: *Meet with ninth-grade learning center to develop action plan. *Post resource maps and other resources on ManateeLearn. *Provide professional development in RTI on PLN and use blended environment for graphing progress in intervention.	Use checklist from the district.	

CHAPTER 6

Exposures to Learning

We recently offered an online professional development module that focused on informal daily assessments. There were presentations, handouts, and professional articles to read in the module. Following are a few comments that were posted in the forum:

> **Kellie Viera**: After reviewing the articles, one assessment that I would like to incorporate into my instruction is the handprint assessment. In this assessment students draw their handprints and in each finger, write one thing you learned today. While it seems more useful with primary students, I believe my students would be engaged in this activity and I could have them use the fingers to assess the various components of the class.
>
> One finger: What did I learn in whole group?
>
> Two: What was most important in small group?
>
> Three: How many questions did I get right on the computer?

Four: What was one important detail from independent reading?

Five: Did I apply myself 100% today?

Kevin Wiggins, social studies teacher: I think this assessment is fabulous. It appeals to the students and engages them in a lot of reflection in a way that doesn't seem overwhelming.

Violeta Velazquez, reading teacher, afterschool tutor for ELL students: Kellie, I also liked this idea and think that I am going to use it. I want to try using it as an exit slip to see how it works with my students.

WHY A PROFESSIONAL DEVELOPMENT FOCUS FOR A PLN?

More than ever, teachers are bombarded with changes in education. Being prepared to teach 21st-century learners requires changes in instructional strategies, use of technology, classroom setup, and other areas. Teachers today are required to have expertise in many areas: student data, technology, pedagogy, content knowledge, and classroom management. Our teachers want to learn, but they often can't find the resources. When they need to know something about a specific strategy or topic, there is not always a scheduled workshop available. Our PLN honors teachers' existing knowledge and differentiates for teachers who are not knowledgeable about specific topics and expectations. The modules are always available, so teachers can access them when they need them and at their convenience.

SNAPSHOT OF PROFESSIONAL DEVELOPMENT ON *OUR* PLN

As we began to consider changes and improvements we needed to make in our professional development programs, we took simple steps to ensure that these programs would provide what teachers needed in order to increase student achievement. We first examined our data, analyzed them, and developed a plan. We tried to ensure that our professional development plans were inclusive, differentiated, and reflective of our school community's needs.

Needs Assessment Analysis

The first step toward improving the professional development offered to our teachers and staff was to carefully consider and analyze the teachers' comments on our needs assessment. The analysis revealed that teachers had some concrete concerns about the professional development being offered to them, as revealed in the following common complaints:

- Not targeted at audience
- Topics not pertinent to what actually goes on in the classroom
- Mandatory attendance, regardless of need, level of knowledge, and interest
- Offered after school, when teachers exhausted or busy
- No differentiation
- Not available at point of need
- One-time "sit-and-get" with no time for extended learning
- No follow-up for implementation questions or deep discussion

We believe these are common problems with the current professional development opportunities offered at many schools.

Here's how the PLN served the professional development needs that surfaced in the needs assessment at our school:

- We post only information that is applicable to the high school classrooms at our school.
- Some professional development has remained mandatory, but attendance at a given time and place is not

always necessary. Our teachers can access the modules at any time, day or night. They can complete them at their convenience and at their own pace. They can view and review the videos, lessons, and activities.

- Differentiation has become easier. If teachers know a lot about a topic, they work on something else or build on existing knowledge. Teachers do not have to sit through presentations on topics about which they are already knowledgeable. They can move quickly or slowly, as their needs, time constraints, and interests dictate. In addition, we have invited teachers to lend their expertise by contributing their knowledge and ideas in the development of modules for professional development sessions in their particular content areas.

Steps Toward Implementation of a Blended Environment

Although submitting electronic lesson plans would prove to be a quick and easy way for teachers to address the district's requirement with regard to lesson plans, some teachers were initially overwhelmed with the process of simply logging on to our PLN, much less writing and uploading electronic lesson plans. This provided us with our first opportunity to begin offering professional development in a blended environment.

We met face-to-face with our entire faculty during the first week of school and demonstrated the process of logging on and uploading lesson plans. At this time we also introduced the content area liaisons as experts to whom the teachers could go to for modeling and help. We created a calendar (also posted) that included blocks of time that were color-coded according to phases of implementation. We developed three phases of expectations for successful uploading of electronic lesson plans. They were

- *Training.* This consisted of both a face-to-face training and an interval afterwards, during which the technology and curriculum coordinators and content area liaisons were available for meeting with the teachers in small groups or one-on-one for direct, explicit, face-to-face time for additional demonstrations and modeling. Office hours were noted on a calendar for each person, each day.

- *Implementation.* This was an interval during which teachers could try to independently submit plans or seek help. This was also a time to troubleshoot and resolve problems encountered. Content area liaisons were available to help.
- *Application.* This was the actual deadline for independently submitting electronic lesson plans. Teachers were responsible for having mastered the process by this date, having had ample time for modeling, practicing with support, and independent practice.

We had 100% of our faculty submit electronic lesson plans successfully by the application deadline. Subsequent data indicated that some of the reasons for our success were

- *Leadership.* Setting up tiered leadership teams gave ownership to many before beginning the official training phase. The departments had a voice in each of the lesson plan templates, the technology committee created the explanatory documents, the content area liaisons were designated as leaders with expertise, and the administrative team supported all the efforts. We had built a strong and broad foundation of knowledge before introducing it to the entire faculty.
- *Usefulness.* Submitting electronic lesson plans was a nonnegotiable, a district mandate, for our entire faculty; therefore every teacher was required to know how to upload lessons. This added authenticity to the usefulness of the training; it wasn't just going to be something the teachers could leave the session and forget about.
- *Support.* Providing concrete and explicit objectives (calendar, phases of implementation) and steps for success

Figure 6.1	Training, Implementation, and Application Schedule

Training	Implementation	Application
August 18: Introduction to ManateeLearn August 26 @ 1:00 auditorium (all) Demonstration August 27 – 28: Robin/Laurie/ content liaisons (hours on calendar) available to model/ help/troubleshoot August 28: deadline to log on to ManateeLearn to check password, attempt to submit lesson plans Sept. 1: administrators to contact those who failed sign on ManateeLearn Sept. 2: content area liaisons available for help 1:00 – 2:00 Sept. 3 – 4: Robin/Laurie available to help & model Sept. 4: all faculty to have attempted to submit lesson plans for second 2 weeks (September 7 – September 18)	Sept. 8: administrators to contact those who failed to submit lesson plans electronically Sept. 9 – October 2: Robin and Laurie available to troubleshoot (office hours). Oct. 1 – 2: Robin and Laurie available to troubleshoot (first 20 minutes of each class)	Oct. 5: 100% of faculty successfully submits complete lesson plans electronically

(a document on how to upload lesson plans) and posting these for all to have easy access to for learning and review eliminated teachers' anxiety about expectations and requirements. Providing scaffolding for teachers who needed additional face-to-face training gave the teachers who needed it the extra support they needed, but we also honored teachers who did not need additional training by not requiring all to attend.

- *Follow-up.* Building in accountability increased the willingness of teachers to attempt to log on and upload lesson plans. We set up our PLN so that the uploaded lesson plans went directly to each department's administrator. The administrators provided electronic feedback on the plans submitted and sent follow-up e-mails to teachers who failed to submit lesson plans.

Using professional development as a segue to introduce our faculty to our PLN guaranteed success because we were able to scaffold those who needed it in the blended environment and familiarize our entire school community with how each individual could navigate our site to best meet his or her needs.

Initial Electronic Uses of Professional Development on PLN

Because we have a blended environment for our professional development, our sessions are both face-to-face and online. The initial introduction of the online professional development component of our PLN was new to many teachers, so we moved slowly, offered additional face-to-face support, and tried to meet diverse needs. Following are the details of how we addressed each of these areas.

Technology

Using an electronic PLN was a new concept to the majority of our stakeholders, including teachers and administrators, so this was a natural place to begin the process of teaching and learning for our school community. We started with the instructions for logging on and uploading lesson plans, but as the interest and participation in ManateeLearn grew, so did the requests for more technology training. Our technology committee, including both experts and novices, began to work on posting resources and information for the teachers and administrators on a variety of topics, including designing websites, using Excel, how to optimize use of Elmo visual presenters in the classroom, and instructional uses for iPads.

Schoolwide Goals

Because we provided resources and ideas for kickoffs in the professional development section of our PLN, teachers felt supported, and many accessed and used the resources. The initial focus for kickoffs was text structure. Some teachers knew all about text structures and did not need additional support, while other teachers had no idea what text structures were or how to use instructional strategies to explicitly teach them. By posting ample resources (including videos, handouts, explanations, graphic organizers, content-based examples, and links), teachers who needed support could access it. Teachers who did not need extra help were not required to use it.

Conferences

Because budget shortfalls have become commonplace, conference costs have led to decreased participation in conferences outside our district. We set up a folder entitled *Conferences* under our professional development link. Teachers who attended a conference could upload presentations, handouts, reference lists, and a summary of the best lessons learned into the folder.

Trends and Mandates

We also use the professional development link to post information and resources with regard to current and upcoming changes in education. Although our school was not required this year to create a massive amount of documentation with regard to Response to Intervention (RTI), many of our teachers were interested in learning more about it but simply didn't have the time to search for the information themselves. We developed a module that included details about all aspects of RTI. We simply posted the module for teachers to access at their leisure if they had interest. There were no announcements, requirements, or expectations. Eleven teachers accessed it and went through entire module, taking about an average of about two hours to complete it. As we acquire more information and resources, we can simply add them to the module.

Earning Points Toward Recertification

After speaking to representatives of professional development in our district, we developed a specific plan to create some modules that could be completed for points toward recertification. Our teachers showed interest in and a preference for using the PLN to access and complete modules. As a result of this interest, we recently created and posted an online professional development module entitled Common Board Configuration, which focused on the use of engaging kickoffs and informal daily assessments. The participants received 3 hours of credit toward recertification for completion. We had 69 teachers sign up to participate.

A BIRD'S-EYE VIEW OF PROFESSIONAL DEVELOPMENT ON *YOUR* PLN

1. Design a professional development plan that addresses your school's needs. Collect and analyze your data to determine the areas in which professional development is needed. The members of your leadership team should be selected so as to ensure a broad base of knowledge on that team prior to beginning; you should have more than one person who is knowledgeable and can help facilitate the process for those who may need additional support. Build support and follow-up into your plan.

2. Make it useful. Don't provide only theoretical and research-based information without linking it to the classroom. The information provided should somehow translate to better instructional practices and increased student achievement.

3. Use the introduction to the PLN as a first opportunity for learning. Regardless of the topic you choose for your school's introduction to the professional development portion of your PLN, an easy first step is to teach the teachers how to access your site, using a blended environment for your modeling and demonstrations. Feel free to use our expectation phases if they will help you as you begin to plan your professional development calendar.

4. Be inclusive. A PLN is an inclusive platform. While you are developing opportunities for teachers to learn, keep in mind that the entire faculty and staff should be able to access each module and learn from it. Invite all to participate. There are never too many people for the space! There are no longer bad times either, as participants can access the opportunities at their convenience.

5. Purposefully differentiate. Give teachers options with regard to topics, modules, and levels they choose to complete with each learning opportunity. If a teacher has expertise in a particular area, perhaps he could become one of the leaders who provide face-to-face scaffolding for teachers who are not yet confident with online learning.

6. Offer continuing education credit when possible. Offering credit honors teachers' time and effort, and serves an overarching goal of improving practice and while maintaining certification according to your state's requirements.

REVIEW

Regardless of your school demographics or level, professional development is always an important part of increasing the pedagogical expertise of your teachers. Here are some things to remember as you begin to consider what professional development opportunities should be offered at your school.

- Ask teachers what they want to learn, and then provide it to them.
- Honor teachers' learning by providing differentiated topics and information that they need in their professional practices.
- An increase in teachers' knowledge about teaching practices and content can lead to increased student achievement. There is no limit to the number of modules you create and post for teachers at your school. Availability of resources and ease of access increase the probability that teachers will use them.
- Create authentic learning opportunities that can be translated into improved classroom practice.
- Provide support for all learning. Include scaffolding by experts, build in face-to-face intervals for teachers who would benefit, and follow up with professional conversations and additional resources.

CHAPTER 7

Begin Your Focus With Eight Steps

WHAT ARE THE STEPS YOU NEED TO BEGIN?

Now that we have discussed the building blocks of constructing a PLN, the first step is to get started. There are eight basic steps to follow to build a successful PLN to benefit your school community. You can use Resource L as a guide to these eight steps. Remember, utilizing a PLN is an ongoing process that doesn't end with Step 8. Evaluating and revising your process is necessary if your PLN is to continue to be a useful tool.

Step 1: Put Together Your Learning Leadership Team

Step 2: Gather and Analyze Student Data

Step 3: Identify Mandates, Curriculum Needs, and Professional Development Needs

Step 4: Select and Build a Technology Platform

Step 5: Identify Content Area Liaisons

Step 6: Develop a Timeline for Faculty Training, Implementation, and Accountability

Step 7: Evaluation and Reflection

Step 8: Revisions

SNAPSHOT OF THE EIGHT STEPS TO BUILD *YOUR* PLN

Step 1: The Learning Leadership Team

As discussed in detail in Chapter 3, the learning leadership team is the foundation of the PLN. By blending face-to-face and web-based support, the built-in layers of leadership meet the needs of the faculty and staff, ultimately leading to higher student achievement. As indicated in the diagram below, the learning leadership team works closely with the principal. They then communicate directly with the content area liaisons, who in turn offer support to the faculty and staff. The team should be kept small and should be willing to gather advice from the content area liaisons when considering decision making.

The learning leadership team should agree on a time and place to meet regularly. During the initial phases of creating the PLN, this team should meet weekly to get the product off the ground. In the meeting, the administrator should work with the curriculum coordinator and technology specialist in moving on to Steps 2 through 5 of the plan. This planning stage is crucial when selecting the right PLN for your school environment.

At times, the principal may be the administrative representative on the professional learning team. Among the advantages of this arrangement is that an open dialogue with the principal takes place in regularly scheduled meetings. It is also helps to add a certain weight to the PLN, as teachers and

Figure 7.1 Tiered Leadership Structure: Learning Leadership Team

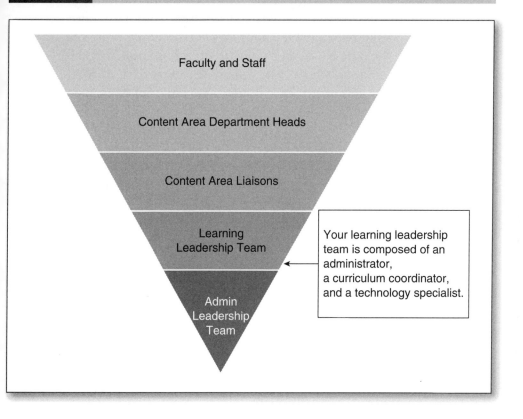

faculty will often notice the principal's involvement; this will in turn increase the buy-in. At other times, the principal may choose to receive feedback and updates from the learning leadership team without actually taking part in the meetings. The advantages of this include the ability to meet more frequently or for longer periods of time. In either case, the principal needs to be kept involved in the process and must be able to offer ideas and solutions.

The curriculum coordinator plays an important role in the learning leadership team. The coordinator's role could take the form of a separate position funded by the district or school; in this case, the coordinator would have the ability to assist teachers full time. If budgetary reasons do not allow for this, the curriculum coordinator could be an administrator at the school site who is in charge of curriculum. The coordinator needs to be knowledgeable about best instructional practices as well as the data gathered from student information and the faculty needs assessment. They should also be able to train teachers in large settings or in one-on-one environments. Due to the responsibilities of the other members of the learning leadership team, the curriculum coordinator will do a large amount of the training. This person should be a well-respected member of the school community and should have the desire to work with teachers to assist their learning curve in mastering the PLN.

Finally, the technology specialist is responsible for building the technological component of the PLN. The technology specialist must have a strong background in technology as well as a background in training teachers. Along with the curriculum coordinator, this person will be doing a large amount of training and assisting.

Ideally, the technology specialist will be available full time to build the PLN. However, in many cases schools do not have the resources to hire a full-time technology specialist. If this is the case, it is important to offer one teacher extra planning time to build the PLN. The amount of time available to the technology specialist is crucial in determining what type of PLN your school should utilize. In the early stages of building the PLN, the technology coordinator will consider the recommendations of the administrative representative and the curriculum coordinator in designing the PLN. In the later stages, gathering information on how the teachers use the PLN will help to direct some of the instructional design.

Step 2: Gather and Review Student and Faculty Data

All pertinent data must be analyzed, and school goals must be set. This process might have already been carried out by the school's leadership team, in which case the administration should disseminate this information. If this has not occurred, student data, including grades, test scores, and discipline and attendance records, must be gathered. Data must also be collected that represents the teacher demographics, years of experience, and teacher needs as identified through a needs assessment survey. Finally, data should be collected regarding the technology available on campus and the comfort level with using technology among the staff.

Step 3: Identify Mandates, Curriculum Needs, and Professional Development Needs

After the team has been developed and the data collected and analyzed, it is necessary to consider national, state, or local mandates before moving on and finalizing any decisions. In addition to mandates, the curriculum—for example, whether there is a common curriculum that must be followed or certain benchmarks that must be met— must be considered. It is unwise to make final decisions without making arrangements to adhere to both the mandates and the curriculum. As educators, we are responsible for respecting the decisions made at the federal, state, and local levels. While the PLN can be altered to meet the ever-changing mandates that arise, at first all consideration should be given to fulfilling current mandates. Doing this will help ensure stakeholder support.

In addition to meeting the mandates at every level and preparing for future mandates, the data can also provide key information for identifying professional development needs. Taking into account what professional development is desired and needed by the staff to fulfill schoolwide goals will help in making some of the decisions required in building the PLN.

Step 4: Select and Build a Technology Platform

Before any decisions are made, creating a list of what technologies are available is essential. It is natural to want to build the most glamorous PLN that can be created, but it is more important to build one that can be sustained, not only by the people who will use it and run it, but also by the technology that will support it. The system must be safe and secure for users. Decisions must be made on where the information will be housed, either locally or on an outside server, and how users will log in safely and securely. Furthermore, proper arrangements should be made to guarantee that the system can grow over time and not collapse from growth. Working with the technology specialist and a team of support personnel will keep the system operational and sustainable.

Step 5: Identify Content Area Liaisons

In Step 5, the content area liaisons are identified. In this step, it is important to choose a few individuals from each content area to be represented. Explaining the purposes of the PLN in relation to the schoolwide goals will be important when recruiting these content area liaisons to help in supporting the faculty. It is important to look for faculty members who have a strong foundation in their subject area and are comfortable working with the learning leadership team as well as with members of their departments. The content area liaisons will be a strong link between the developers of the PLN and its users.

Step 6: Develop Timeline, Faculty Training, Implementation, and Accountability

A timeline that reflects your projected goals and the time you have to spend on building your PLN should be developed and then communicated to the faculty. This helps set expectations and creates a clear path for the future. Equally important, when goals on the timeline are met, a moment should be taken to thank all those involved in order to help keep the process moving. If goals are not met, the timeline may need to be revised after an evaluation is done to determine why the goals were not met. Tracking your pace is key to a successful PLN.

| Figure 7.2 | Tiered Leadership Structure: Content Area Liaisons |

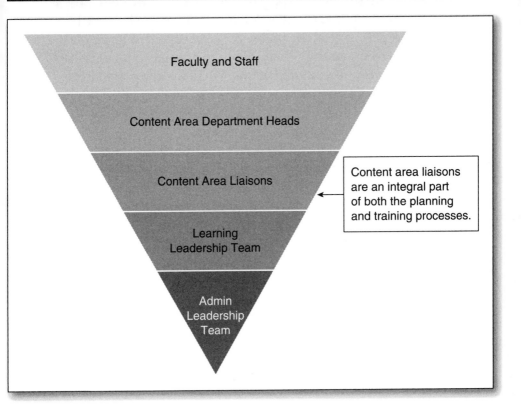

Step 7: Evaluation and Reflection

Several methods can be used in any evaluation process. The benefit of technology is that there are always reports that can be run to view how users are using a system. These *back-end* data (user information that a hosting website or web-based platform records) are extremely useful and should not be ignored. To uncover the backend data of your PLN, work closely with the technology specialist who will in turn work with the platform provider to demonstrate how to run reports. Often PLN users will say that they are using a system one way without realizing that they also use the system for other methods, such as simply checking the school calendar or referring to a past resource used in a professional development setting. Backend data should be a part of the evaluation process.

A second method of collection information can be done by keeping a running log of problems that arose during implementation or use of the system. Content area liaisons can help in this process by communicating what their specific areas saw as benefits or concerns. The learning leadership team can also take ongoing notes in the areas of leadership, technology, professional development, or curriculum.

The combination of all these items, plus other information obtained by students and other stakeholders, can be used for reflection and to help in the revision process. As you will see in Step 8, the revision process is just the beginning of reforming and perfecting your PLN.

Step 8: Revisions

Taking into consideration the evaluative information provided in Step 7, revisions can be made by the learning leadership team. In order to make sure the revisions will be effective, information should be taken from the PLN, then taken into consideration as the learning leadership team carries out the PLN revision process that starts with Step 2. In other words, the PLN is constantly changing. Revisions and evaluations must be ongoing in order to meet the needs of students and staff. It could be that your PLN is ready to grow beyond its current purpose, and you will need to expand how you utilize the tool to support your school community.

REVIEW

By utilizing this eight-step process, you can start building your PLN for your school community. The easy worksheet (Resource L) will guide you in starting to narrow your focus and selecting your team. When you start to plan for your PLN, remember some of these key points:

- The learning leadership team, once formed, will make Step 2 of the plan a manageable task.
- Once data are gathered and content area liaisons are selected, then the real bulk of the work begins by building a useful collaboration tool that will aid in communication, support curriculum, and expand teacher-driven professional development.
- Don't give up! It wasn't too long ago that we too started at Step 1 with an idea and then continued to focus forward as we developed a successful PLN.

All of the resources described and presented in this book are also available at www.your professionallearningnetwork.com.

Resource L

*Creating a Focus: Eight Steps to
Building a Successful PLN*

❑ Put together your learning leadership team
- o Administrator: _____
- o Curriculum Specialist: _____
- o Technology Specialist: _____
- o Other Representatives in Areas of Weakness: _____

❑ Gather and review student data and faculty data
- o Top Three Student Needs:
  - 1. _____
  - 2. _____
  - 3. _____
- o Top Three Faculty Needs:
  - 1. _____
  - 2. _____
  - 3. _____

❑ Identify Mandates, Curriculum Needs, and Professional Development Needs
- o Mandates: _____
  _____
- o Curriculum Needs: _____
  _____
- o Professional Development Needs: _____
  _____
- o Available Technology: _____
  _____

❏ Select and Build a Technology Platform
  o Moodle
  o Google Apps for Teachers
  o Wiki/Blog
  o E-mail System
  o Website
  o Other

❏ Identify Content Area Liaisons
  o Math: _____
  o Science: _____
  o Language Arts: _____
  o ESE: _____
  o Electives: _____
  o Social Studies: _____
  o Small Learning Communities/Academies: _____
  o PLCs _____
  o Other: _____

❏ Develop Timeline: Faculty Training, Implementation, and Accountability

❏ Evaluation and Reflection
  o Faculty/Staff Survey
  o Student Data
  o Data from Other Sources

❏ Revisions
  o Improvements to be made:

  _____

  _____

  _____

  _____

CHAPTER 8

Adding Perspective

*Viewing a PLN With
a New Lens*

A REVIEW OF WHY A PLN

As it was mentioned in Chapter 1 of this book, our initial goal in creating a PLN for our school was to provide a platform from which to articulate and communicate the school's mission, vision, and goals to all community members. Student achievement can be raised only by building in the proper support structure. In order to move from good to great, classroom instruction must be the focus. Developing common routines and a common language that molds the culture of the school is a pivotal step. The creation and implementation of ManateeLearn allowed our school to do just that; as a result, the path to student achievement has been paved. In this chapter, we will discuss our achievements and what we took to be our next steps on the path to improved student achievement.

A Snapshot of Our Experience

With the introduction of the PLN, we hoped to gain an understanding of what our faculty needed to raise student achievement schoolwide. We narrowed our focus; set attainable, measurable goals; and pursued these goals in the ways described in this book. We used faculty surveys, as well as other faculty and student data, to set these goals. We also monitored the system to determine just how the system was being used. For example, when we noticed that teachers wanted to review the resources listed under the professional development section, we decided to add to this resource to meet the needs of our faculty.

To measure achievement, it is important to review the original objectives. To do this we revisited the goals we set for Year 1. These goals were outlined in Chapter 1 and are presented here as well:

Year 1: School Level

- Design a PLN that addresses specific needs of our school community.
- Familiarize teachers and administrators with an educational management system and provide scaffolding for the technology skills needed to use our PLN successfully.
- Have each teacher use our PLN regularly for online collaboration and asynchronous learning and sharing of information.
- Populate folders so they will be useful in providing sample lessons, lesson plans, sample student work, presentations, graphic organizers, professional development resources, departmental kickoffs, and other useful materials.
- Provide a go-to area for access to new national, state, and district mandates and access to secure student data.
- Unite professional learning communities within the school environment to support common schoolwide goals.

In Year 1, we were able to design a PLN that addressed the needs of our school community. Furthermore, we worked diligently to train teachers on how to use the system. Teachers were supported through regular training sessions in short increments to allow them the time they needed to grasp the concept of a PLN. We also created compelling reasons to log in to ManateeLearn, ranging from paperless submission and review of lesson plans to accessing curriculum resources and a school calendar.

Perhaps one of the greatest accomplishments was the development of the resources associated with the various subgroups on ManateeLearn. As previously mentioned, the professional development section became useful, not only in providing asynchronous information to teachers, but also in supporting our face-to-face training sessions and meetings. Where at first teachers were directed to go to ManateeLearn to read materials, they now simply go there first to check for information before seeking it elsewhere. Teachers also now have a place to display their expertise, creating further buy-in and ownership from the faculty.

At the end of Year 1, we looked ahead to Years 2 and 3. We noticed that in several instances we had moved past our Year 1 goals and were set to accomplish Year 2 goals before the end of Year 2. This success can be credited to the preparations we took before building ManateeLearn and to the strong dedication of our faculty. By basing our decisions on data we gathered about our students and our faculty, we formed a strong foundation for success.

In addition to what we set out to accomplish, we also had several accomplishments that were not a part of the original plan. In surveying a portion of our faculty, we were able to see that the majority of users wanted to simplify the processes of submitting lesson plans and accessing important links. These two items are what drove users to the site, so we knew in Year 2 that we needed to address these two areas to keep the users coming to the site.

We also found that the faculty's comfort level with technology was increasing. In a faculty survey, we discovered that the majority of our faculty would still like to see face-to-face learning, but one third of the faculty would prefer to take a web-based professional development course. This increase is an important trend to monitor, because web-based courses can be more cost effective for school districts and at the same time more convenient to educators.

In our efforts to raise the comfort level with technology, we discovered that teachers wanted the ability to access training materials before and after the training. Looking at use of the PLN platform, we were able to track who viewed the materials. This helped us to analyze the training sessions and the faculty's interest in applying the materials to their teaching practices. If there was a particular set of materials in high demand, we offered further supplements. Figure 8.1 illustrates one week when teachers voluntarily reviewed supplemental materials after a face-to-face training session. The end of the week fell on Saturday and Sunday, but during the week the materials were reviewed on the teachers' own time.

Finally, one of the greatest accomplishments that we discovered dealt directly with student achievement. As part of meeting adequately yearly progress (AYP), we track the lower 25% of our student population for growth. These students often require differentiation within the classroom as well as support outside of the classroom. We offer various tutoring programs and intensive reading and math courses to raise the achievement of these students. Before the establishment of ManateeLearn, we noticed that this was not a schoolwide effort; in order to support the lower 25% of our student population, we needed to make it a schoolwide effort. ManateeLearn helped accomplish that. We implemented a mentoring program that allowed teachers to pair with a student for support outside of the classroom. Through the use of the PLN, teachers were given materials to help in coaching students. Student data were also collected and stored, allowing teachers to view their students' progress.

Figure 8.1	Professional Development Resources (screenshot)

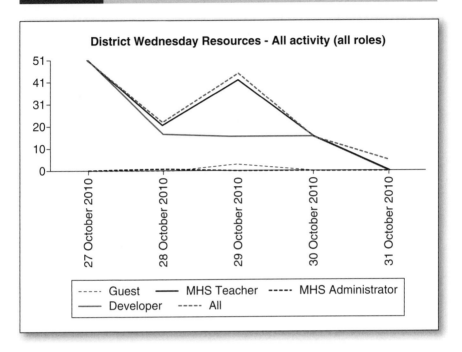

THE FUTURE OF PLNs

The concept of a PLN is new. We were very successful in the first year of implementation. We plan to continue to revise and rework ManateeLearn to meet the ever-changing needs of our school community. As mandates change and testing requirements are altered, a strong system of support and communication is vital in order to meet the challenges. However, we know that this is just the beginning. So as we review Year 1 and move forward to Years 2 and 3, we are beginning to work toward a learning network that not only helps our faculty and staff but also aids the students and parents. As we work to streamline our curriculum, we want to offer a way for parents and students to feel supported. To really raise rigor and relevance, we need to lift the bar, both at school and away from school.

Working within our learning leadership team, we look to increase the effectiveness of our learning network by including a separate area for student and parent support. By adding in this layer, we can reach students both inside and outside the classroom in a "one-stop-shop" type of site. Our school website acts as a method of communication to the community, which is important; however, the website is not designed or intended to support instruction. Utilizing the PLN to support academics offers another avenue to improving student achievement.

Currently, many teachers have their own websites. This is a positive step, but it is not enough. Teacher websites vary, and every time a student visits a teacher's website, he or she must become accustomed to that site's design. In addition to lacking a common structure, there are teachers who do not have the skills needed to produce their own website or the time to update one. By using a learning network, some of this responsibility can be shared among a group of teachers who teach the same subject. In other words, one location can be used for students and parents to bridge the gap between the classroom and the home. Students and parents could review information before it is taught in the classroom, allowing for extra support if students need it. There are many possibilities for developing a PLN that offers students the ability to review notes, download assignments, and communicate asynchronously. We hope to begin building this for our students in the near future.

THE FUTURE OF *YOUR* PLN

We have designed a model PLN at the site http://www .yourprofessionallearningnetwork.com that you can use as a basis for the design of your own site-based PLN. With this book as your guide and the website to assist you, you will be able to implement a successful PLN at your school and merge your school community with the future.

References

Conley, J., Sherry, M., & Tuckey, S. (Eds.). (2008). *Meeting the challenge of adolescent literacy: Research we have, research we need.* NY: Guilford Press.

Curry, M., & Killion, J. (2009). Slicing the layers of learning: Professional learning communities fill the gaps as educators put new knowledge into practice. *Journal of Staff Development, 30*(1), 56.

Danielson, C. (2009). *Talk about teaching: Leading professional conversations.* Thousand Oaks, CA: Corwin.

Dede, C., Ketelhut, D., Whitehouse, P., Breit, L., & McCloskey, E. (2009). A research agenda for online teacher professional development. *Journal of Teacher Education, 60*(1), 8–19.

Donavant, B. (2009). The new, modern practice of adult education: Online instruction in a Continuing Professional Education setting. *Adult Education Quarterly: A Journal of Research and Theory, 59*(3), 227–245.

Hord, S. (1997). *Professional learning communities: What are they and why are they important?* Austin, TX: Southwest Educational Development Laboratory.

Hord, S. (2009). Professional learning communities: Educators work together toward a shared purpose. *Journal of Staff Development, 30*(1), 40–43.

Hord, S. M., & Hirsh, S. A. (2008). Making the promise a reality. In A. M. Blankstein, P. D. Houston, & R. W Cole (Eds.). *Sustaining professional learning communities.* Thousand Oaks, CA: Corwin.

Hur, J., & Brush, T. (2009). Teacher participation in online communities: Why do teachers want to participate in self-generated online communities of K–12 teachers? *Journal of Research on Technology in Education, 41*(3), 279–303.

Kane, S. (2007). *Literacy and learning in the content areas* (2nd ed.). Scottsdale, AZ: Holcomb Hathaway.

Kao, C., & Tsai, C. (2009). Teachers' attitudes toward web-based professional development, with relation to Internet self-efficacy and beliefs about web-based learning. *Computers & Education, 53*(1), 66–73.

Knight, J. (2009). Coaching: The key to translating research into practice lies in continuous, job-embedded learning with ongoing support. *Journal of Staff Development, 30*(1), 18–20.

Marzano, R., Waters, T., & McNulty. (2005). *School leadership that works: From research to results.* Alexandria, VA: Association for Supervision and Curriculum Development.

Peterson, C. (2003). Bringing ADDIE to life: Instructional design at its best. *Journal of Educational Multimedia and Hypermedia, 12*(3), 227–241.

Sawchuk, S. (2008). Sites mimicking social networks set up for staff development. *Education Week, 28*(1), 1.

Sheehy, P. (2009). Give your professional development a Second Life. *Technology & Learning, 29*(7), 28.

Signer, B. (2008). Online professional development: Combining best practices from teacher, technology and distance education. *Journal of In-Service Education, 34*(2), 205–218.

Stoll, L., & Louis, K. S. (2007). Professional learning communities: Elaborating new approaches. In L. Stoll & K. S. Louis (Eds.), *Professional learning communities: Divergence, depth, and dilemmas,* pp. 1–14. Berkshire, UK: Open University Press.

Vavasseur, C., & MacGregor, S. (2008). Extending content-focused professional development through online communities of practice. *Journal of Research on Technology in Education, 40*(4), 517–536.

Weil, M. (2008). Summertime: "To do" list—a look at the different ways to tackle training and development programs that offer big rewards once the school year starts. *Technology & Learning, 28*(10), 33.

Westerberg, T. (2009). *Becoming a great high school.* Alexandria, VA: Association for Supervision and Curriculum Development.

Index

CORWIN

A SAGE Company

The Corwin logo—a raven striding across an open book—represents the union of courage and learning. Corwin is committed to improving education for all learners by publishing books and other professional development resources for those serving the field of PreK–12 education. By providing practical, hands-on materials, Corwin continues to carry out the promise of its motto: **"Helping Educators Do Their Work Better."**

Advancing professional learning for student success

Learning Forward (formerly National Staff Development Council) is an international association of learning educators committed to one purpose in K–12 education: Every educator engages in effective professional learning every day so every student achieves.